PERFECT PHRASES™

for

OFFICE
PROFESSIONALS

**Hundreds of Ready-to-Use Phrases
for Getting Respect, Recognition, and Results
in Today's Workplace**

Meryl Runion and Susan Fenner

New York   Chicago   San Francisco   Lisbon   London   Madrid   Mexico City
Milan   New Delhi   San Juan   Seoul   Singapore   Sydney   Toronto

The *McGraw·Hill* Companies

4 5 6 7 8 9 10 11 12 13 14 15   QFR/QFR   1 9 8 7 6 5 4 3

ISBN   978-0-07-176674-6
MHID   0-07-176674-X

e-ISBN   978-0-07-177054-5
e-MHID   0-07-177054-2

This book is designed to provide communications information and guidance. The publisher and the authors do not offer legal or other professional services. Every effort has been made to offer advice that is accurate, sound, and useful. Results vary in different situations. Please use your own discretion in applying these phrases. The authors and the publisher cannot be held liable or responsible for any damages caused or allegedly caused directly or indirectly by the information in this book.

Library of Congress Cataloging-in-Publication Data

Runion, Meryl.
    Perfect phrases for office professionals : hundreds of ready-to-use phrases for getting respect, recognition, and results in today's workplace / Meryl Runion and Susan Fenner.
        p.   cm. — (Perfect phrases series)
    ISBN 978-0-07-176674-6 (pbk.)
    1. Business communication.   I. Fenner, Susan W.   II. Title.

HF5718.R86 2011
651.7—dc22   2011008413

McGraw-Hill books are available at special quantity discounts to use as premiums and sales promotions or for use in corporate training programs. To contact a representative, please e-mail us at bulksales@mcgraw-hill.com.

This book is printed on acid-free paper.

              in Everyone   123

              Perfect Phrases to Promote Interdepartmental
              Communication   125
              Perfect Phrases to Get Office Members to
              Work Collaboratively   126
              Perfect Phrases to Encourage and Empower Office
              Members to Be Self-Sufficient   128
              Perfect Phrases to Address Company Layoffs
              and Terminations   129
              Perfect Phrases to Manage Emotions   131

Chapter 13   Perfect Phrases to Speak for Your
              Manager   133

              Perfect Phrases to Get Your Manager to Authorize
              You to Speak on His or Her Behalf   135
              Perfect Phrases to Get Your Manager to Stop
              Undermining Your Authority   136
              Perfect Phrases to Get Your Manager to Credential
              You to the Rest of the Office   137
              Perfect Phrases to Get Others to Come Directly
              to You   138
              Perfect Phrases to Gracefully Inform Someone of
              Your Manager's Mistakes   140
              Perfect Phrases to Make Your Manager
              Look Good   141
              Perfect Phrases to Address Complaints and
              Criticisms About Your Manager   142

Foreword

My role as executive director of OfficeTeam gives me a good sense of what distinguishes the most effective administrative professionals. Office professional responsibilities have expanded dramatically in recent years. The businesses we work with seek professionals who stretch beyond their job descriptions, juggle multiple priorities, and address unexpected and urgent matters. Many managers now turn to their administrative teams for help controlling costs, troubleshooting technology, planning meetings and events, and even evaluating potential hires. It's a new world. What does that mean for you?

You need to be able to form partnerships with your managers and the staff you support in order to communicate and work with them on complex and creative assignments. You also must be self-assured and assertive in requesting opportunities to grow your skill set and to ensure your ideas are heard. That takes excellent communication skills.

According to OfficeTeam's exclusive research among support staff and senior managers, solid communication skills are vital for career success. In fact, 81 percent of human resources managers polled by OfficeTeam, HR.com, and the International Association of Administrative Professionals said verbal communication was the soft skill in greatest demand at their firms. Knowing just what to say and when to say it makes a difference. Actually, one could argue this makes *all* the difference.

Effective communication is simple in theory but difficult in practice. In fact, it can be downright messy. Sometimes, it's difficult to get the right words across from one situation to the next.

What's an office professional to do?

Meryl and Susan have simplified the process with phrases throughout *Perfect Phrases for Office Professionals*. The phrases communicate confidence and competence as they invite collaboration.

The most successful office professionals I've worked with embody these qualities. They've shown confidence by assuming ownership of an assignment and seeing it through to completion. They've also learned my work style, the questions and concerns I'm likely to have, and the way I prefer to communicate.

Since 1991, OfficeTeam has been on your team, providing free tools and resources to administrative staff, helping them excel in their roles and advance their careers. We proudly support Administrative Professionals Week every April and sponsor the annual Administrative Excellence Award, which recognizes the performance of outstanding office professionals across North America. Meryl Runion and Susan Fenner are on your team, too, and have created a resource that will help you communicate in the new world of office professionals.

As you read this book and begin using the phrases within, keep the following in mind: When you're a confident, collaborative communicator, you're at the top of your game. And you'll help keep your managers at the top of theirs, too.

—Robert Hosking
Executive Director of OfficeTeam

Preface

I'm All About Empowered, Collaborative Communication

"Hearing you speak last year saved my job," Clarissa told me after inviting me to speak to the admins for her school district. "My boss had already told me we'd never have a good working relationship. After I heard you speak, I decided to prove him wrong and did."

Suddenly it all felt worth it.

I've spent close to twenty years gathering, developing, and sharing information to help administrative assistants like Clarissa speak effectively. The world is full of training courses and books telling managers and leaders how to communicate for results. Office professionals have far fewer resources regarding how to practically address workplace communication challenges. I enjoy filling that gap with my hard-won knowledge.

As a communication speaker, author, and (I like to think) thought leader, I've spoken to more than a hundred thousand businesspeople—professionals who represent tens of thousands of companies and organizations. I've been inside hundreds of corporations, organizations, and businesses. I've gotten direct feedback and anonymous evaluations from the vast majority of people I address. My clients and audiences love sharing their practical wisdom and insight. They don't mind telling me when they find my recommendations impractical. I don't mind asking them what would work better and helping them figure out how to either make my recommendations work or find their own answers. I listen, pen and paper in hand.

I don't work with just administrative assistants. I also work with leaders, managers, and a large assortment of other professionals. I see that as essential. When a manager tells me about a communication challenge with an admin, I've already heard the admin version of the conversation. I can advise the person in ways that incorporate both perspectives. When an office professional asks about a communication challenge with a manager or leader, I've already had the conversation from a managerial and a leadership perspective. Again, I can incorporate both perspectives into my suggestions.

Every now and then, someone will e-mail or write to tell me about how my words helped resolve a situation. This information needs to get out. That's why I proposed this book to my editor at McGraw-Hill and elicited the savvy and wise collaboration of the International Association of Administrative Professionals' Susan Fenner to make it a reality.

You Can Go Cheap for Power or Deep for Empowerment

Some business communication methods teach manipulative tricks, defensive moves, and power plays. It's useful to know how that game is played and how to operate with supposed allies who act more like adversaries. You'll get some of those strategies here. However, my SpeakSTRONG Method is character-based. It teaches you how to respond to adversarial communication without power plays. At his or her best, a collaborative communicator defeats adversarial communication by turning the adversary into an ally. I call that assertive collaboration.

What I love about working with admins and office professionals is you understand collaborative communication. You're used to getting results without wielding power or pulling rank. You're less tempted than some other professionals to go cheap for power. You like the idea of going deep for empowerment. You understand why this style is the best way to get recognition, respect, and results.

Whether it simply makes your job easier or saves your job, as it did for Clarissa, I and my coauthor, Susan Fenner, offer this body of knowledge as a resource for your success. This book provides the tools and phrases for administrative assistants and office professionals to communicate at your highest empowerment level. Let us know how else we can help.

—Meryl Runion

I'm All About Admins: Let Your Voice Be Heard Above the Noise

I am in awe of you! You are the can-do heroes of the office. You are the folks managers rely on to get a job done—any job—because you do it all. You are supportive, rock solid in your loyalty, and fearsome when a challenge is thrown your way. There's no one better when a new technology has to be learned and applied (without warning or training) or a seemingly impossible task is delegated with the expectation that it will be done by the end of the day amid a million interruptions.

You are amazing professionals. And yet you don't realize your power or the enormous scope of your contributions. It makes me sad to see you being less than you could be and thinking too small.

That's why when Meryl asked me to coauthor a book of perfect phrases for admins and other office professionals, I jumped at the chance! I saw it as a way to offer a boost in reaching your personal and professional potential and attaining your career aspirations.

Administrative professionals are near and dear to my heart. Having worked with admins for more than twenty-five years at the International Association of Administrative Professionals (IAAP), I have come to know a lot of wonderful admins, listened to their stories (the agonies and the ecstasies), and watched them blossom into outstanding and remarkable professionals (well above anything they ever could have imagined, even when I saw the seeds within them long before).

As a group, you are so skilled, so capable, and so dependable, and yet you so often fail to recognize your true worth. My mission is to help you use your individual and collective voice to get the respect and backup you have earned. To ask for what you want and need and to stand up for yourself and your profession. To feel like an equal partner on the work team. My mission is to help administrative professionals—just like you—find a voice to impart your true value to your organizations. This book is one resource among many to help that happen. (See the back of the book for suggestions on resources.)

So, dear admin, Meryl and I want you to know that many people "have your back." This book is yet another way to give you, the ultimate office professional, the voice you seek—to speak up when you have a better way or when you feel you're being compromised, left out of the work team, or not acknowledged for being the professional you know you are. The phrases offered here will, we hope, open your mind to what you can do and have the right to do—for yourself and for your profession. It's all there for the taking—and the doing! I'm all about admins. This book is all about you—all for you.

Let us know how it changes your life. We know it will!

—Susan Fenner

Introduction

It's a New World Out There

Wake Up! The Workplace Is Changing

Wake up and smell the changes. As an office professional, you need to stay connected to the latest trends in business and business communication.

Have you noticed? Today's workplace has less staff, fewer resources, and tighter budgets. Planning is shorter-term. Strategies shift overnight. Technologies evolve overnight. Corporate cultures change overnight. To quote one author, someone keeps moving the cheese!

Positions are eliminated while the accompanying work increases. Lean and fast are in vogue. You face greater responsibilities. Managers expect you to turn out more work more quickly. Your work roles, titles, and expectations change continuously. Previous roles, titles, and responsibilities have blended. Nothing is as tightly defined as it once was.

As an admin or office pro, you may now be required to add to the bottom line and mandated to show returns. There is more group work, teamwork, and collaboration. Much of that interaction is with remote workers, contract workers, and telecommuters. There is increased diversity and more global reliance. Office professionals connect directly with customers and clients, both face-to-face and through social media.

Networks form around projects. Colleagues collaborate intensively for short periods and then disband to re-form with new assignments. More generations with different values and styles interact. The official hierarchy is less delineated, and formal structures are dissolving. Your workplace is becoming more casual, not only in dress but also in organization, conversation, and function.

The workforce is burning out from increasing pressures over time—with no end in sight. The lack of job security and the diminishing civility build stress. The stress shows up at home, and people cry out for work-life balance—with promises that next week, next month, next year, we will find it.

Do you get tired just reading this? This is not your father's workplace. It's not even your mother's workplace. Wake up. It's all changing.

Control! Alt! Shift! The Office Professional's Role Is Also Changing, and You Need to Change, Too

Work with the workplace changes and they'll work for you. Resist and you can be taken out at the knees. Shift and you'll survive—even thrive. Remain stagnant and you'll crash and burn. Here are some ways you need to shift as an office pro.

■ **Take on more managerial and leadership responsibilities.** You are not an order taker. Often you're called on to supervise, negotiate, delegate, and train and mentor. You're asked to take ownership of projects and make them successful. Learn how. Stop waiting for direction. Help shape the direction. See what the need is and step in.

■ **Adapt to new demographics.** You may report to a manager (or managers) half your age with half your experience and a very different style from yours. (The opposite could also be true.) If that's an issue for you, get over it. Adapt to your managers' styles, and figure out how to effectively communicate your expertise in ways that respect their cultures and approaches.

■ **Find the balance between structure and the need for speed.** As an office professional and a master of systems and established procedures, you can be a voice for order, structure, and process. However, in the new work environment, speed often trumps quality, and official channels will need to be bypassed to get things out quickly. Represent the balance between the two.

■ **Take ownership for results.** For many salaried workers, being a team member also means being flexible and accessible. While boundaries are necessary, if you're salaried, you may be asked to respond when something urgent hits the fan at "off-hours." Stay aware of what your job description declares your primary function. Balance that with the need of the moment.

If your job doesn't require or even allow you to take work home, your job security still depends on results, so plan ahead. Don't leave people hanging by going home on time without anticipating what needs to happen first and what people who aren't on the clock may need from you before you go. Check in with the team before you check out for the day or the week.

■ **Master the technology of your trade.** Do your tutorials and adopt new technologies before you're forced into it—or, worse, let go for not knowing them. Show your professionalism by staying current with technologies.

Collaborate! The Manager/Office Pro Partnership Is Changing, Too

You and your managers are collaborators in the big game of getting respect, recognition, and results. Here are three ways to succeed at that game.

■ **Partner, partner, partner.** Susan and I use that word deliberately. You have a partnership with your managers now. There's more equality and teamwork. Roles are less compartmentalized, with managers doing more routine work (e.g., booking travel, answering e-mail) and admins doing more complex work (e.g., managing budgets, creating and giving presentations).

■ **Be a team member.** In some cases being a team member means dropping rank and relating as an equal with someone below you on the org chart. In other cases it means relating as an equal with someone above you on the org chart. When you manage multiple managers, make sure your contributions to the team get the respect they deserve (whether or not it translates into increased pay).

■ **Recognize how much you and your managers have in common.** Chances are you share common pressures and opportunities in the changing workplace that may include overwork, job insecurity, burdens of increasing regulations and oversight, outside partners, alliances, sponsors—the list goes on. Your managers travel less, and you may well travel more.

Step up to the plate and collaborate as a partner. Drop the old roles that keep you from contributing as much as you could.

Get Empowered!

Update your communication skills into empowered, effective communication for today's world. The nature of power is changing with changing demographics. According to the U.S. Department of Labor, since 2009, women have outnumbered men in management. Since the fall of 2010, women outnumber men in the workforce overall. That is a significant shift in demographics that changes business as usual. The qualities generally associated with women such as relatedness and collaboration are becoming more the norm in the workplace. The influences of Gen Y, social media, and globalization also affect how power is used and shared.

There are six communication dynamics to adopt.

■ **Be collaboratively assertive.** Express your view with respect. Say what you mean, and mean what you say, without being mean when you say it. Get to the point in a graceful way that augments, not negates, what others say.

■ **Be assertively collaborative.** Speak up to assure that your expertise is considered in matters that affect you or need your expertise.

■ **Personalize.** Get real and get personal in your business communication. Don't hide behind position or procedures. The old saying "It's business; it's not personal" dismisses the relational aspect of communication. Recent trends in business communication lean toward increasingly personalized, engaged, and conversational interactions.

■ **State concisely.** Balance the need to personalize with the need for speed. Get in and get out. Get right to the point and say something significant concisely.

■ **Optimize.** Find the synergy among individual talents, approaches, and styles within each team, group, and unit. Be like the gourmet chef who finds the perfect combination of foods to create a great meal—discover the perfect combination of traits and talents to create great results.

■ **Mobilize.** The social dynamics of our culture demand momentum. Don't block the flow with unnecessary procedure, administrative delay, or nonresponsiveness. Keep things moving. Help others get the momentum they need to succeed.

Don't talk as if today were yesterday. Stay current with business communication trends. That means get empowered and speak up appropriately and skillfully.

Speak Up! Get the Respect, Recognition, and Results You Deserve

Respect, recognition, and results don't happen by accident. They happen by design. Here's how.

Speak in Ways That Earn Respect

To get others to respect you and the job you do:

- Be clear, sincere, and effective. Consider your words before you speak.

- Respect yourself. Don't say things that diminish your stature or professionalism. Speak as the professional that you are. Respond without reacting to managers who neglect to respect you.

- Respect others. This doesn't mean you should put anyone on a pedestal. Just know that people respect people who respect them.

Speak in Ways That Earn Recognition

To get others to recognize you, your work, and your ideas:

■ Make your work visible. Don't whine, but also don't make your job look too easy. Avoid saying things like "It was nothing" in favor of saying things like "It took a lot to make that happen, but it worked!"

■ Ask for recognition when appropriate. Don't be shy about requesting that your name go on your work.

■ Be willing to share recognition when it serves your team, even if the credit isn't evenly earned. Sometimes you'll get more recognition by not demanding credit for every contribution. Often people who don't insist on getting credit for everything end up getting recognized for being valued team members.

■ Give recognition to others. People recognize people who recognize them. Make a point of acknowledging others.

Speak in Ways That Get Results

To make things happen:

- Don't let the desire for respect and recognition interfere with the need to get the job done.

- Clearly ask for what you want from others, and explain why in terms of shared outcome.

- Help others get results. People support people who support them.

Sometimes you have to choose among seeking respect, recognition, and results. Every situation will be different. Ultimately it's about balance.

How to Use This Book

We wrote this book to offer examples of the best words to say what you have to say. Use it to enhance the expression of your own thoughts, feelings, and desires. Use your best judgment to adapt the examples to your personal situation and style. If in doubt, contact HR or your company's legal department.

You can use this book two ways. One is to read it from cover to cover as a practical crash course in effective professional communication. The other is to use it as a reference for a particular situation.

When you select a phrase, make sure it feels right to you. We discovered that some phrases that sounded fine to one of us sounded hokey, dismissive, hostile, or unclear to the other. Some phrases could catapult your associate to success and not work at all for you. Don't assume that because a phrase is in this book, it will get the result you want. Make sure you understand the point and purpose of every phrase, and adapt those that don't fit you or your situation.

However you use this book, let the phrases here lead you to success. Your job has gotten bigger and will keep expanding. We wrote the book to help you meet that challenge with perfect phrases you really can use to grow with your job. We're here to help in other ways as well. Know that the International Association of Administrative Professionals (IAAP) and Meryl at Speak-STRONG have your back and your future!

CHAPTER

1

Perfect Phrases to Establish Yourself in Your New Role

You got the job! What now? Here comes the hard part—establishing yourself with a new exec and a new work team. You want to come across as a professional, without appearing pushy or looking like a pushover. You need just the right balance of assertiveness and willingness to work with other people's styles. After all, you are the new kid on the block.

Remember, it's as challenging for your new office mates to get a replacement admin on board as it is for you to be that admin. They'll wonder how good you are at your job, if you can fill the shoes (big ones, no doubt) of your predecessor, and whether you'll fit in with what they may feel is the best work group ever (or not). They will have some of the same anxieties about you, and about your meshing with them, as you have about testing the waters and finding your place within an existing team. Establish your position deliberately and fix things before they get broken.

This chapter gives you the perfect phrases to introduce yourself to your manager and colleagues. You'll find just the right words to ask about their way of doing things and to tell them what worked well for you in the past. You'll learn how to blend into the group with small talk that opens doors, as well as how to handle the inevitable faux pas (it happens to the best of us). Also, you'll find ways to address comparisons with the person who held the job before you.

It's hard to overcome a bad first impression, so make your initial meeting with your new work team one that gets you accepted and respected and starts your career off on the right foot.

Perfect Phrases to Introduce Yourself to a New Manager

What do you say after hello? Here's what.

→ Hi! My name is [name], and I'm your new office professional (or admin).

→ I expect we'll be busy, so I'll give you the short version of my background.

→ I'm excited to be a member of your team because [reason].

→ I've heard great things about working with you. You know people say [compliment you've heard], don't you?

→ I expect we'll be learning a lot about each other in the next few weeks. I'm so glad I'm here.

→ I'm new to you but not new to the industry. I look forward to supporting you and learning from you.

→ I am so excited to be here— this is my dream job!

→ These first few weeks will be a learning experience for both of us. What can we do to make it all go smoothly?

Perfect Phrases to Forge a Manager/Admin Partnership

The words you use can set a tone of boss/employee or a tone of professional colleagues. These phrases use words such as *partnership* and *team* to establish the new relationship as a partnership. Some managers have never had a partnership-style relationship with their support staff and may resist before they embrace it as valuable and needed.

→ I like partnering with my managers because that's how we get the most done.

→ The reason why I think we're going to make a great team is [reason].

→ I want to be the best office manager you've ever had. Let's talk about how we can be a great team.

→ I was excited to be on this team, and here I am!

→ Every management/admin (or exec/office pro) team (or partnership) is different, so I look forward to seeing how our team will evolve.

→ As your team rookie, I notice [observation].

Perfect Phrases to Relate Your Best Work and Communication Style

While generally the support person expects to adapt more to execs than to have execs adapt to the support person, it is appropriate to let your managers know how to best communicate with you. These phrases will help you tell your manager the best way to interface with you.

→ I work best by [e.g., providing daily updates and having weekly face-to-face meetings, even if they're for only five minutes]. Does that work for you?

→ I like to respond to e-mails in batches. I do that every two hours. For something urgent, if you flag it, I can respond right away. OK with you?

→ I find if I get an overview before I delve into the details, I understand a lot better. Could you explain things for me a bit before you assign them?

→ If you could explain why we do something, it helps me choose the best way to handle it. That way I won't have to interrupt you with as many questions.

→ If we could check in each morning, I'd know I'm making your priorities my priorities. It won't take long—even five minutes would work.

→ If you could summarize the steps you want me to take for tasks, I won't have to guess how you want things. I'd be more likely to get it just the way you want it.

→ I'm a can-do person. Let me know if what I'm doing works for you.

→ I like to stretch myself. If I overstep my boundaries, just tell me. That's how I find out where they are.

Perfect Phrases to Discover Your Manager's Preferred Work and Communication Style

Everyone operates at his or her best in different ways. The system that worked so well with one manager may not work well at all with another. Here are phrases to find your manager's style.

→ What's the best way for me to ask you about [area]?

→ How do you like to be updated on [area]?

→ Is there a messaging system you like?

→ Do you text? Is it a good way to reach you?

→ If I needed something from you right away, how should I contact you? E-mail? Text? Phone?

→ Let me know what I have your authority to handle and what I'll need to run past you first.

→ At the beginning, I'll probably check in fairly often. With time, that should decrease, once I know your work style.

Perfect Phrases to Establish Your New Role with All Levels of Employees

You might have just met your manager, but as his or her admin or office pro, you represent your manager, sometimes with people who know this person much better than you do. These phrases will help you establish that unique role.

→ You know [manager's name] much better than I do. I respect that. However, as her admin, I speak for her now.

→ I know you're not used to having to go through me to get to [manager's name]. It's an adjustment. I'll do whatever I can to be an ally rather than a barrier.

→ I'm still learning what I need to support [manager's name], and I know it seems quicker to go directly to him. In the long run it will be quicker for all of us if you go through me, even if I end up just asking him the same questions you're asking. Thanks.

→ [Manager's name] and I met and decided I'm now going to handle all [area].

→ We've made some changes with my coming on board. I'll now be the one you'll talk to for [area].

→ Here's what I can do for you: [how you'll help].

Perfect Phrases to Collaborate with Other Office Professionals

You can't find a better network than other office pros. They can help you get things done, and you can help them get what they need. These phrases will help establish your mutually supportive relationship.

→ In my last job, the admins got together regularly to network and support each other. Do you do that here? I'd like to set that up if you don't.

→ I'm headed to [department]. Can I get you anything?

→ You and I can make each other's jobs a lot easier. I don't have as much to offer just yet while I'm learning, but I will when I get up to speed. Then I'll do whatever I can to support you.

→ I hope we can share new ways to solve problems. You can tell me what works here, and I can tell you what worked for me before.

→ If I talk too much about how we did things at [previous company], let me know. I love exchanging ideas and figure it's good to share best practices.

→ I want you to know that I'm a team player and will be here when you need me.

→ I'm looking forward to working with you. This is going to be *great*!

Perfect Phrases for Questions About and Comparisons with Your Predecessor

When you're new, you fill someone else's shoes. Whether those shoes are big ones or small ones, these phrases will help you talk gracefully about your predecessor.

→ [Predecessor's name] left for [personal] reasons. I don't feel right talking about it, but you can ask him directly.

→ I'm not comfortable talking about [predecessor's name's] flaws, but I do love hearing what worked for him.

→ Thanks for the compliment. I hope my work stands on its own so we don't need to talk about my predecessor. It's a new game.

→ I know you liked [predecessor's name], and while I don't expect to ever replace him, I do hope to win you over in time.

→ I can see that [predecessor's name] was good at [area]. My forte is [area(s)].

→ A new person always changes the office dynamics. I hope you'll like working with me.

Perfect Phrases to Initiate Meaningful Small Talk

There is nothing small about small talk. Big things start there. These phrases will help your small talk be more meaningful.

→ I was thinking about [reflection that struck you] on my way to work today. Do you ever think about that?

→ One of the things I like about working here is [what you like]. What do you like best about working here?

→ (Notice when someone appears touched by something.) That seems important to you. May I ask about it?

→ How did you get where you are here? What were some turning points in your career path?

→ If you had one tip for me about succeeding here, what would it be?

→ What is the best thing that has happened to you here?

→ What is the most interesting thing that happened here?

→ What is the most exciting thing that has happened to you professionally?

→ What are your goals here at [company]?

→ Is that your [daughter/son/family]? [Comments on family pictures.]

CHAPTER 2

Perfect Phrases to Manage Inevitable Learning Curves

OK, you're hired, you schmoozed with your new manager and work team, and you made a positive impression on your "new BFFs" from nine to five. It's time to learn the ropes in this new setting. You don't know what you don't know—so, how do you navigate your office-rookie learning curve while maintaining some sense of dignity?

Pay attention to this point. Learning curves are inevitable. The secret is to admit that you won't hit the ground running and master all that you did in your old job right away. Susan recalls a job in a new industry and town, doing things that were foreign to her. She was apprehensive, but she knew she could transfer her knowledge and skills to the new setting with time. She figured what she didn't know, she could learn from others *if* she stowed her ego. Though she had been on the top rung of her profession at the old organization, she was starting all over at the bottom in this new job. Susan swallowed her pride, brushed up on her questioning skills, and asked for help when she needed it. People wanted to help and felt good about knowing things she didn't. They saw her as an approachable, appreciative, able comrade who would fit in because she felt comfortable enough to depend on others when she needed them.

Susan teaches from her success. I teach from failure as well as success. I was in over my head in my first admin job and didn't ask for support. I now know that my manager would have supported me had I asked. Instead, I faked it and quit before he discovered my incompetence. I learned a valuable lesson. I don't hide lagging learning curves anymore.

This chapter will provide you with the perfect phrases you need to get oriented in a new position, to clarify what seems muddled, and to find out where you ought to go to get answers to tough questions. It gives you the words you need when you inevitably make a mistake or get in over your head.

Relax and take advantage of this period during which not having all the answers actually works to your advantage.

Perfect Phrases to Ask for Help Getting Oriented

If you aren't greeted with an effective orientation, don't fake it and make stuff up. These phrases will help you get the direction you need.

→ How do new employees find out how things work around here?

→ If you were new here and a little lost, which employee would you talk to?

→ Everyone is so busy that I haven't gotten a detailed orientation. Are there resources I can use to get my bearings?

→ I'm looking for someone to take me under his or her wing and show me the ropes as I get settled in. Would you be willing to do that for me?

→ I have a list of information that was provided to me. Do you see any gaps or things I ought to know that aren't listed?

→ When you need help figuring out how things work, what person do you talk to? Sometimes I feel lost.

Perfect Phrases to Handle Questions You Can't Answer

No one who really thinks about it expects a new admin or office pro to know all the answers. Actually, even seasoned veterans still encounter questions they can't handle. These phrases will help you address what you don't know without sounding incompetent.

→ I don't know, but I'll find out!

→ That's a new one for me. Do you have suggestions about how I can find the answer for you?

→ I'm happy to find out for you. Since I'm new, it may be quicker for you to look it up yourself, but if you don't mind waiting, I'll get your answer for you.

→ I haven't encountered that yet. Would you like for me to find out for you?

→ I could guess at an answer, but I don't want to mislead you. Let me check on that and get back to you.

→ I'll be glad to look that up for you. Where should I look first?

→ That's a new one for me. Is there someone with experience that I can ask?

Perfect Phrases to Let People Know You're New

Most people have patience with people who are new, but they also want their own needs met. Let them know you've just come on board in a way that explains your limitations without sounding as if you're making excuses or you are inept.

→ I've dealt with a lot of things in the week I've been here, but that one is new to me. Let me check.

→ I know how my last company handled that, but not this one. I'll find out for you.

→ I'm glad you asked that. I'm afraid I can't help you with it yet, but I intend to get the information so next time you need help, I'll have an answer.

→ I don't have that answer for you, since I'm new to the position, but I'll put it on my need-to-find-out list. I'm sure it will come up again in the future.

→ I'll need to check with someone on that, since I'm a newbie. Can I get back to you this afternoon?

Perfect Phrases to Request More Detailed Explanations

People often assume you're more up to speed than you actually are. These phrases will help you ask for more detailed explanations.

→ I appreciate the overview. Can you fill in a few blanks for me?

→ I have a vague picture, but I need more details to move forward. I don't know enough to know what to ask. Can you help me figure out what details I still need?

→ Let me repeat what I think I heard you say: [your understanding].

→ You want me to do [your understanding]. Is that correct? Did I miss anything?

→ Is there a version from last year that I can use as a model?

➔ Since I'm new, is it OK if I do a rough draft and get back to you to make sure I'm on the right track?

➔ Can I do a mock-up and run it by you before I spend a lot of time maybe focusing on the wrong things? I want to do my best with this project!

Perfect Phrases to Clarify Office Jargon

Everyone has his or her own way of saying things. Office jargon is automatic, and you may need to ask more than once for people to "speak plain English." These phrases will help you decipher the local acronyms and other unique usages.

➔ What does [e.g., "ConW"] mean?

➔ I know what that meant at my last company, but I'm not sure that it means the same thing here.

➔ Can we have a session where you fill me in on all the office jargon you can think of?

➔ Is there a list of most-used acronyms? If there isn't, I'd be glad to make one. It would help me and other new hires.

➔ I'm developing a list of words and abbreviations specific to this office, so I can follow you better. What should I start with?

➔ Every time I hear a word or an abbreviation I'm not familiar with, I'd like to ask you its meaning. Is that OK with you?

Perfect Phrases to Get Support from People Who Know Your Job

The best people to get help from are those who have either done your job (or parts of your job) or worked with people who did. These phrases will help you tap into their knowledge and experience.

→ I've learned I can save lots of time by asking people who have actually done what I'm trying to do. Can you walk me through this?

→ What did you like about how [predecessor] did this?

→ How would you do this if you were I?

→ I'll develop my own style, but in the meantime, while I'm learning, if you see me do anything inefficiently, will you let me know?

→ I'm trying to learn how you do it here. Can you steer me in the right direction?

→ Before I put a lot of time into this, will you take a look to make sure I'm on the right track?

Perfect Phrases to Admit Mistakes and Look Good in the Process

"I made a mistake" is a powerful phrase. Admit mistakes with humility, but don't self-depreciate. To err is human. To admit err is divine. To ignore or hide errors is dangerous. These phrases will help.

➜ I just found out what doesn't work.

➜ That wasn't the result I was going for.

➜ Can I have a do-over?

➜ This is what I would call a learning experience.

➜ I won't make that mistake again!

➜ I know I won't make that mistake again because next time I'll [better approach].

➜ My bad. My lesson.

➜ Yikes! I really goofed that up. I'll know better next time!

➜ What was I thinking! Whatever it was, I'll get it right next time.

Perfect Phrases to Admit You Are in Over Your Head

No matter how good you are or how experienced, there will be times when you just aren't capable of doing what others want you to do. When—new or seasoned—the responsibilities you're charged with simply are over your head, these phrases will help.

➜ I've never used that [technology/format/application] before. Can you give me a quick run-through so I can see it being used and write down the steps? Then I can do it just the way you want it done.

→ I think I've bitten off more than I can chew with this additional assignment. Can we renegotiate deadlines?

→ I thought I could do this myself, but I can see that I'll need to get some help from [name/resource] if I don't want to hold you up. Is that OK with you?

→ I'm totally new to [e.g., Twitter] and know that I am expected to use it to [purpose]. Where do you recommend I go to get up to speed?

→ While doing [task], I came to an application I never used before: [e.g., manipulating the financial data the way you asked me to]. Can you recommend a good online tutorial?

→ I was and am qualified to do the job you hired me for, but I confess, there are some new elements that are difficult for me. I need some help.

→ As much as I'd like to whip out this assignment for you, I have to admit that I've never done it this way before. I'm trying to learn many new processes and meet the deadline. Can we talk?

Perfect Phrases to Apologize Without Groveling

When you do something you would never deliberately do again, it calls for an apology. Go ahead and say you're sorry. Just don't grovel when you do it.

→ I'm sorry.

→ I didn't intend to do that.

→ I regret that [error].

→ How can I fix this?

→ What would it take for me to make this right?

→ Please forgive me.

→ When I [action], it [negative effect on the other person]. I see that now, and I'm very sorry.

CHAPTER 3

Perfect Phrases to Establish Communication Agreements

Admins and other office professionals often complain that their managers don't tell them where they're going or that they don't get a heads-up when a major work project is coming their way. They complain that it's easier to get an act of Congress than arrange a meeting with their execs. It can take multiple requests to get a single answer, or they have to ask other managers what their own manager is up to in order to stay in the loop.

As an office pro, you may ask four questions and get one answer or put a project on hold for three days while you wait for a thirty-second response once the exec finally focuses on it. Once they do get a response, admins and office pros may need to guess at the manager's meaning. It's also common to be bypassed on requests regarding projects the admin or office professional handles, as well as to be left out of meetings and decisions that affect them.

When we hear admins complain about these things, we'll ask what the managers and other associates say when the admins address the issues. The response often is: they never brought it up.

You may be lower on the organizational chart, but if you're not getting the kind of communication you need to do your job well, everyone loses. Your entire team depends on you to see yourself as a professional and create collaborative communication agreements that keep the flow of communication running smoothly. The phrases in this chapter will help you have conversations about communication lapses. They will lead to the establishment of solid communication agreements that will enable you to do the job you were hired to do in alignment with other office activities. Instead of complaining about ineffective communication, be proactive and ask for mutual agreements about how you can better communicate with each other. Agreements help everyone stay in sync.

Perfect Phrases to Establish Communication Agreements with Your Manager[1]

When you ask for communication agreements, ask in a way that makes it clear those agreements will help you better support your manager(s).

→ I'd like to establish some basic communication guidelines so our messages will be more efficient and things run more smoothly.

→ I've found that when my managers and I agree on how we're going to communicate, things flow better.

→ I want to be the best admin you've ever had, and if we establish how we'll communicate, that will help a lot.

→ We all have different ideas of what good communication is, so I'd like to get us on the same page about what it is for us.

→ Communication agreements are like setting rules of a pickup basketball game before we start. They help make sure we're playing the same game the same way.

→ I may not realize that I haven't explained something completely. If you're missing important information, please ask. Agreed?

→ If something I say isn't clear, please insist I clarify.

→ I'm sensitive, but I do want to know if something I say or do isn't right. Promise you'll tell me?

1. For sample communication standards, see www.speakstrong.com. For free communication standards poster downloads, see www.speakstrong.com/freestuff/stds-resp-com.pdf.

→ If I catch a mistake, how do you want me to tell you?

→ Sometimes we can use the same words but have a different intent or meaning. If it seems to either of us that we aren't really communicating, let's stop and find out where it went wrong. OK?

→ When we e-mail each other, let's bullet separate points, mark questions, and update the subject line. Does that work for you?

→ If you need an immediate response, the best way to communicate with me is to [e.g., flag the e-mail/put a note on my desk]. How do you want me to handle urgent items?

→ Do you like using a Blackberry, text, e-mail, phone call, [other example] best to communicate with people? Will you teach me how to use any new tools I may not be familiar with?

→ How do you like for me to ask questions? A phone call, a drop-by, an e-mail?

Perfect Phrases to Establish Communication Agreements Within Work Groups

Establishing standards within work groups isn't very different from establishing them with your manager. However, you may play a larger role in defining what the agreements will be, depending on the nature or your relationships.

→ I find that establishing communication guidelines helps things stay on track. Here's what's worked for me: [procedure]. Do you have anything to add that works for you?

→ If you need an immediate response, the best way to communicate with me is to [procedure].

→ I make a point to respond to e-mails and voice mails within twenty-four hours. Can you agree to do that, too?

→ Let's talk about what we want more than what we don't want—and what would work more than what isn't working. That way we won't sound as if we're complaining to each other all the time.

→ If we can't deliver on promises, let's offer our reasons but never give excuses. Are you cool with that?

→ I have codes I like to use in e-mail subject lines—things like TR for task request and Q for a question. Are you open to using them?

→ If you change the topic of an e-mail thread, will you please change the subject line too? That will help me track and file your messages.

Perfect Phrases to Arrange for Regular Meetings with Your Manager(s)

Regular meetings can be of high value. They also can be hard to get. Ask in a way that will make your manager want to make you a priority.

→ How often would you like to meet?

→ I'd like us to meet [weekly/monthly] and update each other [frequency] in between. Does this sound like the right amount of time to you?

→ I find that if I have a regular meeting with a manager, it keeps me from having to interrupt during the day as much.

→ In order to make sure my priorities are your priorities, I'd like to meet [frequency].

→ I respect how many things you have on your plate, and I don't want to distract you. If we meet for quick morning and evening updates, I'll know I'm tracking your priorities without having to interrupt your train of thought.

Perfect Phrases to Assure That You Are Consulted on Decisions That Affect You

When decisions affect you, your input can make the difference between success and failure. Ask for that input.

→ Before you commit my time, could you talk to me briefly, just to make sure it won't jeopardize a higher priority?

→ Your priorities are my priorities, and I can complete them more efficiently if you check in with me before anything is set in concrete.

→ I can help you factor my work into the deadlines for the [name] project so I'll be available to give you the support you need when the project reaches my desk.

→ Before you decide about [project], can I look it over? Sometimes a simple request such as using a particular format can take the team a few seconds and save me hours of administrative time.

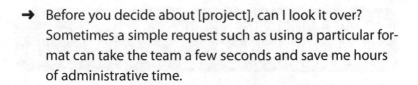

Perfect Phrases to Discuss Solutions to Communication Breakdowns or Confusion

If there are communication snafus, ask to debrief them and decide how to avoid them in the future.

→ I thought I had the specs on that project, and it turned out I didn't. That caused hours of wasted time. I'd like to see how we can make sure the specs are clear to me next time. I suggest [idea].

→ There were a few communication snafus yesterday that I'd like to avoid in the future. Do you have any ideas how?

→ Wow! We really had a miscommunication disaster yesterday. Let's talk.

→ I might have misheard you when you [e.g., gave instructions]. From now on, I'll try to repeat back what I hear so we'll be on the same page.

→ I'd like to figure out why I interpreted your request so differently from what you intended. Can we review and debrief our conversations from yesterday?

Perfect Phrases to Explain Special Communication Needs

If you have a disability that requires some special accommodation, ask for what you need. At the same time, know that it may take reminding, since your request requires people to change old habits. Don't get angry, but don't sacrifice a genuine need, either. Get support from HR and senior management to formulate appropriate accommodations.

→ I can read lips really well if you're facing me when you speak. That helps me make sure I'm hearing you right. Can we make sure we talk face-to-face?

→ I can't see your lips right now. I need to see them to understand.

→ I appreciate how gracefully you accommodated my special needs. It'll help me do a great job.

→ If we could [accommodation], it would save me lots of time and energy. Would that work for you?

→ I've found that [accommodation] helps me be more efficient, since it [benefit].

→ I have trouble with [challenge due to special need]. [Accommodation] levels the playing field for me. I know it's a shift.

Perfect Phrases to Adapt Communication Modalities to Preferred Styles

Are you primarily auditory, visual, or kinesthetic? In other words, do you like to hear, read, or be shown? While the office professional certainly needs to adapt to the preferred styles of others, it's perfectly acceptable for you to ask for information in modalities that work best for you, too.

→ Could you write out those instructions for me?

→ This would be clearer for me if I could watch you do it first.

→ Can you sketch a picture of what the finished product would look like for me?

→ I'd like to watch you do this before I attempt it. That helps me remember what to do when I'm on my own.

→ I can tell that you are a visual person. I do better with verbal instructions. We may have to cross styles to get the job done right.

→ I'll take notes as we talk. I remember things better when I see them.

→ I'd like to repeat back my understanding of what you tell me. That helps me make sure I get it and also anchors the information in my mind.

Perfect Phrases to Select the Best Communication Technologies

There are so many communication modalities these days. Each has its strengths and limits. Determine the one that is best for each person and situation.

→ If a request is really detailed, please e-mail it to me rather than leave a voice mail.

→ We need to interact a lot as we collaborate on this project. What instant messaging program do you use?

→ When an e-mail is more than a paragraph, I think it's time to pick up the phone and talk. Make sense to you?

→ If you ever get frustrated with me, come see me or pick up the phone to talk about it.

→ I can see this is getting complicated. We'd better plan a face-to-face meeting.

→ Your last e-mail left me thinking I've angered you. Do we need to talk about it?

→ I'm calling because e-mail doesn't seem to be working too well right now.

→ Let's include in the subject line what you're supposed to do with the information: FYI, requires action—that kind of thing. Will that work?

Perfect Phrases to Get the Focused Time You Need

Everyone is so busy these days that it's common to have a request ignored. Or you may find that a message that you have taken pains to craft is merely scanned, and the response you get makes it clear the other person did not take the time to focus on what you asked, said, or noted. Ask for the focus you need.

→ I understand you're busy. This is too important to sandwich in between other concerns. I'd like for you to take the time to respond to each point today so the project won't be held up. OK?

→ I have five questions and need five answers. Will you be sure to respond to them all?

→ Sometimes it works to discuss my report while dealing with other issues. This time I need more complete attention.

→ A half hour of your complete attention can save me two days. May I close the door and can we ignore e-mail?

→ If we take the time to do this accurately now, we won't have to make the time to fix it later.

→ I know you're busy, but if you'd give me three minutes, we can complete the specs and move on.

→ I put "Urgent" in the subject line because I need an immediate answer on this. Thanks—I appreciate it!

→ I'm calling to give you a heads-up. In another thirty minutes, you'll have the [project] to [proof/complete]. I'll need it back by [time] to get it out the door by [time].

CHAPTER 4

Perfect Phrases to Manage Managers

Part of Susan's mission at IAAP and my mission at Speak-STRONG is to help admins and other office professionals claim their professionalism. We regularly remind them to respect the fact that while they may not be in the corner office, they have their own unique skill sets and specialty areas that their managers need. One of those skills is to manage managers.

It is not your job to take everything your manager dishes out whether it makes sense or not. It is not your job to tolerate inappropriate or unethical behavior. You weren't hired to be an obedient order taker. It is not your role to stand by silently, watching your manager make mistakes. It is your job to be the office professional you are. That can mean correcting your manager, addressing issues, and presenting ideas.

Managers need to be managed. Managers need help focusing on priorities. Office professionals make their managers' priorities their priorities, and when managers lose sight of those priorities, office professionals have both the expertise and the mandate to help them focus on first things first.

Part of managing your manager involves ensuring seamless relationships with staff and associates. Often, as an office pro, you have more contact with vendors and support staff than the manager does. That means you are in the best position to help manage those relationships.

The key for all of these phrases is to trust yourself and your own professionalism.

Perfect Phrases to Correct a Manager's Mistakes

We all make mistakes. Those of us in the know realize that admitting the mishap and quickly recovering is the best solution. All the same, correcting the mistakes of others, especially those in more powerful positions, takes finesse. Here are your phrases. Tread lightly if necessary, but if your manager doesn't mind your stating directly that he or she made a mistake, just say it.

→ I took the liberty of dealing with a couple of grammar slips.

→ I noticed two numbers that didn't seem right, so I checked them against the report, and they were off. Do you want to see the changes, or are we ready to go?

→ I believe the client lives in [e.g., Palo Alto] and not [e.g., San Francisco proper]. Want me to check to be sure?

→ I rearranged a few of the bullet points for a better chronological flow. See if it reads better for you.

→ I heard you tell [employee's name] that the meeting was Tuesday, but [meeting organizer's name] sent us a memo canceling it. Want me to get back to her before she schedules it on her calendar?

→ I typed up your minutes, and then I added a chart of who does what by when. I think there was a little confusion that this will clarify. See if that helps the assignments stand out. Shall I circulate it?

→ I reformatted the report as you requested and got all the verbs in agreement. It's ready to be sent.

→ I think you might have given [name] the wrong figures. Want me to check to be sure?

→ I'll be glad to check this over with a fine-tooth comb and fix anything needing fixing.

→ Let's compare these numbers with the auditor's report. I know you'll want to be accurate.

→ I found some mistakes. Do you want me to correct them and show you, or just correct them?

Perfect Phrases to Get a Manager to Admit Mistakes

We all have a sense of ego investment in our work. That said, the worst kind of professional is one who sees only what he or she wants to see, even if it's in error. Here are phrases to get your manager to admit mistakes without losing face.

→ I'd like us to have the kind of relationship in which we both admit our mistakes. Does that work for you? I'll let you know when I goof up if you'll do the same.

→ Some managers seem to be concerned that if they admit mistakes, their admin will broadcast it. I assure you, I don't do that.

→ I make plenty of my own mistakes and would tell you if I made this one. It's important to know what really happened so it won't happen again.

→ I could see why you might have made that mistake, since [e.g., everything changed so quickly].

→ This didn't seem to work. What are your thoughts? If we do it again, what would you change?

→ I didn't feel good about the process. What can we do differently?

→ Let's do a postmortem.

→ Let's learn from this experience. Any suggestions? What worked? What didn't?

Perfect Phrases to Break Bad News to a Manager

The old phrase "shooting the messenger" can still apply today. Here are some ways to deliver bad news without getting "shot" in the process.

→ I have good news and bad news. Let me tell you the good news first.

→ Let me start with the easy-to-fix items.

→ I knew you'd want to know this before it hit the office grapevine.

→ The results aren't what we expected, but we can still work with them.

→ I just heard back from [name]. It isn't what we had hoped for.

→ Something happened that you need to know about.

→ If I were in your position, I'd want to know this. That's why I'm telling you. We've come across a snag.

→ You can't win them all, and unfortunately, we struck out here.

→ We lost the battle, but we won't lose the war.

Perfect Phrases to Organize Your Manager

Many managers are go-getters who keep their eyes on the deal, the outcome, and the final figures. They may not be so interested in the day-to-day organization that helps them get their jobs done successfully. That's why they need you on their team. Admins are master organizers. Here are some perfect phrases for getting your manager better organized and primed to focus on high-priority items.

→ You're the idea guy; I'm the organizer. I can help you plan and execute if you'll let me track and organize.

→ What's not working for you that I can make better?

→ Let's share e-schedules so we both can track when you arrange meetings and not double book.

→ You have a meeting coming up next week. Let me know what you'll need, and I'll start compiling now. No need to panic the day before.

→ Here's a spreadsheet I started in order to track [project]. It's guaranteed to make your life easier.

→ I'd like to help you get organized bit by bit so it won't be disruptive. Here's how I'll go about it: we'll start with [e.g., creating folders for e-mail]. Once we've completed that, we can [next step].

→ I can help you get organized without changing your style to do it.

→ I started color-coding your files by project. This should help you move items into the proper places when you're through reading a report or contract.

→ I created red folders for urgent projects. (Once the manager is accustomed to that) I created blue folders for [category] projects.

→ If you'll send me the important e-communications, I can file them so we can quickly find them and clean up your in-box.

→ If you copy me on all the important project components, I can sort, file, label, and format so we can see things at a glance and not have to wade through lots of correspondence.

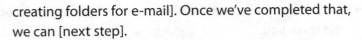

Perfect Phrases to Get Your Manager to Learn and Use the Latest Technologies

Admins are the primary technology users in most companies. They are proficient in a variety of software applications and know how to adapt them to specific work functions. Here are tips for bringing your manager up to speed technologically, while reducing your workload and making you both more productive.

→ I can save you two hours a day. Want to know how?

→ There's an application that will allow us to [function]. Let me show you.

→ I know that [software] still works for you. The problem is the interface.

→ It sends a signal of unprofessionalism that we're still using [outdated technology].

→ I suggest we get [software]. Here's what it can do for us.

→ I reserved a half hour this afternoon so I can walk you through the new financial software.

→ Watch me do this. You'll want to use it too once you see how easy it makes your life.

→ Here are some computer shortcuts (laminated reference cards). They're the CliffsNotes of technology. Next time you get lost, you'll find the answer here.

→ I've put together a how-to computer book with samples. This will make it really easy for you to use the process the company now requires.

Perfect Phrases to Challenge Questionable Decisions

No one bats 1.000. It's impossible to make correct decisions 100 percent of the time. The best we can do is recognize poor choices, own up to bad decisions, regroup, and repair. When you see a questionable decision coming from your manager, you have the right and the responsibility to challenge it . . . of course, by using the perfect phrase.

→ As I read this over, it occurred to me that [concern].

→ Have you considered this angle? [Alternative.]

→ Another way to look at it is [alternative].

→ It occurred to me that there may be a missing piece of the puzzle.

→ So, If we did [action], then would [questionable outcome] happen?

→ I like your plan—a lot. The one worrisome part to me is [concern].

→ Would you like to look at parts A and B again before you submit this? I noticed that [observation].

→ Can I play the devil's advocate?

→ Want me to try to knock a few holes in it—to get you ready to defend this to upper management?

→ I can see the logic in this, and in the short term, it's a good decision. Long term, I see the following issues.

Perfect Phrases to Get Your Manager to Make You Look Good

You and your exec have a vested interest in making each other look good, but not all execs think in terms of an admin's career. Here's how to get your boss on board to help you get the credit you deserve.

→ I'd like to get credit for this in my annual review.

→ Can we have both our names on the project, since I did so much of the work?

→ I appreciate your acknowledging my contributions. I worked hard on this report.

→ I want to keep growing professionally. Getting credit for my share of this project is important to me.

→ I make you look good; you make me look good. That's how it works!

→ We're a good team. Thank you for noting my contributions.

→ It means a lot to me that you [action].

→ I have your back and you have mine.

→ When I look good, you look even better, since you're my manager.

→ When you put me down to others, it makes us both look bad. If you have some issues with me, please bring them to me directly, and talk about me respectfully to others.

→ If you could let [higher-up] know that I [achievement], it could really help my career.

Perfect Phrases to Summarize Information

In today's workplace, the most valuable commodity is time. As they say, time is money, and money is the bottom line in a tough economy. Whatever you can do to optimize your manager's time will also optimize your worth to the company and to your exec.

→ I can give you the short version in five minutes if you will give me your full attention now.

→ Let me start at the end and work backward. Stop me if you have questions.

→ I know you like the bottom line, so let's start there.

→ I've provided an executive summary for you.

→ This [chart/graph/matrix] gives you the bird's-eye view.

→ I've boiled down the information to four broad categories with bullets.

→ I've indexed the material so you can go right to your areas of interest.

→ I've organized the data by [feature]. This should help you when you do the analysis.

→ I abstracted the material for you.

→ I created a list of website links with descriptions that will take you directly to the information you're looking for.

→ I read the material and highlighted the pertinent points, as you asked.

Perfect Phrases to Get Your Manager to Prioritize Your Work

It's been said that you can have it all, but you can't have it all at the same time. The ability to effectively prioritize is a top skill for managers and their admins. Here are some words to use to get your manager to order your work schedule so you'll know how to tackle the top-drawer assignments.

→ Would you rate this as a high, medium, or low priority?

→ If I take on this assignment, what shall I put on hold?

→ We can't do it all at the same time. What shall we label as number one, number two, and so on?

→ On a scale of one to ten, where do you see this project falling?

→ I have four tasks on my immediate to-do list. Where would you like me to sandwich this in?

→ Where would you like me to place this among all the projects I have going on?

→ Here's a list of all my assignments. Will you prioritize them, with one being the first-to-do, highest-priority task?

→ I can see that this project will take [number of hours]. What would you like to take a backseat so I can start right in on this?

→ All these assignments look important. Which one takes the number one spot?

→ I'm going to start with [project] until I hear back from you. If I don't hear back from you, I'll assume that's correct.

Perfect Phrases to Suggest That Your Manager Ask for Help

Who hasn't been in over his or her head at one time or another? The answer? No one! It happens to the best of us! When this happens to your manager, these phrases will soften the impact of suggesting that the manager get help outside his or her area of expertise.

→ We haven't done this before. I suggest we find someone who has, to start us out right.

→ Why do execs think they have to do everything alone? This is exactly what you assembled a great team to help you with.

→ They say two heads are better than one. Shall I get a second opinion to be sure we're on the right track?

→ I'd like to run this by my IAAP colleagues—to see how this is handled in their companies.

→ This doesn't feel right to me. What do you say we get another impression?

→ I'd feel more confident if we had a model to use that has already proved itself to be successful. Agree?

→ If someone were to say, "These areas seem weak," how would you respond?

Perfect Phrases to Get Managers to Manage Rather than Abdicate

Most of us hate confrontation and other parts of our jobs that require us to get out of our comfort zones. For better or for worse, it's all part of getting the job done and necessary for maintaining peace and productivity in the office. Here are phrases to get your boss off the dime and on to dealing with the tough stuff.

→ The team would address the [issue], but it's your job, and we don't want to step on your toes. Can you address it or give us authority?

→ We all like it that you don't micromanage. But there are some situations brewing now that need more direction than we're getting.

→ It's great to empower us to make our own decision. But we're kind of like a team of cats now—going in different directions. We need a master plan.

→ The laissez-faire method of managing works great when everyone knows what to do, but right now the team is waiting for your direction.

→ Here's what I've tried that doesn't work. It's time to call in the top guns . . . you!

→ You're the one with the expertise. What direction do you want us to take here?

→ I can't read minds. I need some direction to do the job the way you want it done.

→ To get the team moving in the right direction, we need you to [action].

Perfect Phrases to Give Advice to Managers

The true professional welcomes opportunities to provide input and change the course of a project or task to move it in a more positive direction. To get good results and have others accept your suggestions, speak in positive, supportive ways. Here are a few phrases to get your ideas accepted, applied, and applauded.

→ In my experience, [opinion].

→ I've seen [observation] work well.

→ Would it improve the outcome if we [idea]?

→ Can I take your idea and build on it?

→ I've noticed that other managers have had good luck by [approach].

→ Looking at it from the other side of the fence, I'd say [suggestion].

→ Can I share my thoughts?

→ If it were up to me, I'd [idea].

→ I've been around you long enough to know how you think, and I have enough distance from this to see things you may miss. Can I make a suggestion?

→ Having learned from the master—you—I suggest that [idea].

→ Here's another viewpoint: [suggestion].

CHAPTER 5

Perfect Phrases to Manage Multiple Managers

There was a day when most admins reported to one manager. That day is long gone. These days, if an admin or other office professional supports only three or four managers, colleagues think the admin has it easy. Could I have possibly heard it correctly when an admin in my audience said she was responsible for the schedules of five hundred managers? Just to be sure—and encouraged by the gasps of the rest of the admins in the audience—I asked her to repeat her claim. I'd heard her right.

Communication agreements, established policies, and clear job expectations are important when there is only one manager. They are vital when you have many. When the numbers reach five hundred, there's no fooling around. The office professional needs to take the initiative to make sure everyone is on the same page about roles, how people will work together, and how to best manage your time and priorities.

Perfect Phrases to Clarify Your Role in Multiple-Manager Relationships

It's your job to make sure your role as an office professional is clear to you and all your managers. These phrases can aid you.

→ Since I support several managers, I want us all to get together and clarify my role. I want to avoid being caught in the middle of different expectations.

→ While I never like to decline a request by saying it's not my job, we all need to agree on what my job is so I don't have to do that.

→ I want to support all of you the best way possible. Let's look at common situations and agree on what that means.

→ When [manager] is out of town, I still have work I do for him. I'll do what I can for you. I just need for you to know I'm not as free as I may look.

→ Uh-oh. I'd like to help you with this project, but as it stands, [manager] has to approve any projects I take on other than hers.

Perfect Phrases to Get Multiple Managers to Collaborate When Delegating

Everyone thinks his or her project is a high priority—and it is, to that person. When you are doing work for several managers, you need to have guidelines established by the group so that you don't get caught in the middle.

→ Have you talked to [name] about that project? She has me doing several things. I'd like for the two of you to decide what I should make my first priority.

→ It would be more efficient if you talked to [manager] directly about giving priority to your project. I can't change his deadline. He has to make that call.

→ I know better than to get between you and [manager] on this. Talk to each other and let me know what you decide.

→ I don't want to speak for [manager], but looking at your project, I think you and she may need to talk. It seems you may be working at cross-purposes and could make more headway if you coordinate your efforts.

→ There's only one of me, and there are five of you. You'll have to talk to the others to be moved ahead in the queue.

→ I'd like to do this for you, but there are three assignments ahead of you. I'll be glad to move you ahead of the others if you get them to agree.

→ I don't make that decision. Ask [manager] for his approval.

Perfect Phrases to Get Multiple Managers to Agree on Your Priorities

You're all on the same team, so get your managers to prioritize your time as a team.

→ [Manager A] thinks my priority should be [item]. [Manager B] thinks it should be [item]. I won't even get started on what [manager C] thinks. I can implement the criteria I set, but it's important for our team that you get together and agree about how you will share my time.

→ OK, let's make a list of how everyone would want me to prioritize my time. Then we'll get real about it.

→ Here's how I suggest I prioritize. Speak now or forever hold your peace—or at least until we can meet again.

→ Aren't we all a part of a team? It seems to me we should be able to agree about how to use my time to serve the bigger mission.

→ I can give you a rough idea as to the number of hours each of these assignments will take. Then you all can decide in what order you'd like me to tackle them.

Perfect Phrases to Address Late, Inaccurate, and Incomplete Projects

You don't want to come across like someone's mother or a schoolteacher. And yet you have the right and the need to let people know that timeliness and quality are interconnected. You're not there to do other people's jobs for them.

→ I'm here to support you, and I want to do that. However, I need you to proof your work before you give it to me. It takes me twice as long if I have to be sure that what you submit is correct.

→ When I turn something in with errors, it reflects on us both. I'm happy to correct the errors that I find, but it's not a good use of my time for me to research your numbers. To make sure the report is 100 percent correct, please check your numbers before you give It to me.

→ Since I get things last, I feel responsible for the ultimate quality of the report. I appreciate it when all my managers get things to me in as complete a form as possible so I can do my part without spending time correcting one person's project.

→ When I need to fill in the blanks on your project in order to be able to turn it around, I'm really doing your job as well as mine. Please take the time to tie up the loose ends before you give it to me. We'll both come out ahead.

→ The deadline for this was [time]. I'll do what I can to meet your schedule, but since I support other managers, I can't drop everything I'm doing for them to get this out today.

→ I'm sorry. I'm getting this late, and there are so many errors to correct and so many gaps to fill in as submitted that the earliest I can get it out will be tomorrow. The work will take about [estimate] hours.

Perfect Phrases to Get Yourself out of the Middle of Multiple-Managers' Conflicts

It's natural for managers to have conflicts with each other. It's also natural for them to want to talk with their office pro or admin about it. Don't get caught in the middle—especially if you report to the manager they're complaining about. Here are some phrases for you.

→ I'd like to help you, but since I support [name] too, it would be better for you to talk to someone else about this.

→ It's natural for you to have issues with other managers. I'd think there was something odd if you didn't. It's natural—but the details aren't my business.

→ I suggest you talk to [other manager] about this.

→ My policy is to only have conversations about other managers that I wouldn't mind their hearing. I don't feel comfortable with this discussion.

→ Let me know how the two of you resolve the issue.

→ That's something for you two to figure out. I don't have any comments.

→ I wish I could shed some light on this situation, but you'll have to talk to [manager] directly to get the full picture.

→ I respect you all and won't put myself in the middle or play favorites. It's not fair to ask me to referee, which is what you're doing when you ask me to take sides.

Perfect Phrases to Address Managers Who Bypass the System

When managers try to shortcut the system, say something. There may be occasions to cut slack, but don't tolerate shortcuts to the extent that the whole system crumbles.

→ I'd like to skip a step or two myself. Let me tell you why it's not a good idea here.

→ Does [other manager who would care] know that you're [shortcut]?

→ You're the manager, and it's your call if you want to go around the system. I just need to point out that there are potential complications in doing that.

→ I'll be glad to do that with a sign-off from [manager].

→ The group decided on [the system]. I can't change that decision without the full group's OK.

→ If I did that for you now, it would set a precedent that would jeopardize the way work flows here.

→ I developed a sign-in sheet for all my work assignments. That way I can give you accurate estimates of turnaround based on my work schedule.

Perfect Phrases to Clarify Communication Pathways Among Multiple Managers

If managers aren't keeping each other in the loop, say something. Here are your phrases.

→ Does [name] know about this?

→ I talk to all of you every day, so I know who needs to know about different things. I suggest you copy [name] on this.

→ I believe [manager] wants you to go through her instead of coming to me directly.

→ I don't mind delivering a message to [name], but I think it would be better for you to tell him directly.

→ Let's call [manager] and ask him right now.

→ I can e-mail [manager] and see if she approves this change.

Perfect Phrases to Handle Confidentiality with Multiple Managers

While your managers generally will share information among themselves, there will be times when you are privy to information that is not general knowledge. These phrases will help you manage confidentiality.

→ Since I support [manager] as well, it may be better that you not give me this information.

→ I can see why you'd like to know about that. If I could tell you, I would. I suggest you ask [manager] directly. I owe her my confidentiality just as I owe it to you.

→ If I told you that, would you trust me with your private information anymore?

→ I'm sorry. I've been told I can share that information only with those directly affected.

→ Part of my job is maintaining confidences. This is one of those times; I have nothing to say.

→ I'm sorry. That information is confidential. You might ask [manager] for more details.

→ I imagine they would tell you if you asked directly. It's not my call to make, though.

CHAPTER 6

Perfect Phrases to Deal with Sticky and Unethical Situations

"Don't make me come back there!" That's the famous phrase parents use when children squabble. Sometimes bad behavior requires action. As a professional, you have ethical standards to maintain. It is not a part of anyone's job description to suffer put-downs or undermining behavior, nor is it part of your job to break the law.

We get what we tolerate. And if we tolerate inappropriate behavior for too long, it can erode our own esteem. I think of Emily, who had a wonderful, supportive manager for thirty years. When he retired, she found a new position with a manager who managed by put-downs. He had no tolerance for the inevitable learning curve that comes with a new situation. After only two weeks with this man, Emily started to question her own abilities. She left. Her replacement stayed—and quickly taught her manager how to treat her.

I think of Mindy, who complied with her manager's request to notarize his wife's signature on some financial papers without her being present. That was the last time she—or anyone else at the company—ever saw her manager. She heard tales of his having moved to Mexico with another woman with the money he stole from his wife, thanks to her complicity.

I think of Sharon, who applied partnership funds toward her manager's private venture and barely escaped being a codefendant in a lawsuit.

These women worked for small businesses that did not have the advantage of an HR department to go to for support. Most large organizations have resources set in place to protect employees. If your company does, use it if you have any concern at all about handling the situation yourself. If things get sticky, it will help if you went through the proper channels. If you don't have an HR department, talk to someone with an HR background and research your situation before taking action.

The phrases in this chapter will help for situations you can handle on your own.

Perfect Phrases to Address Disrespectful Manager Behavior

Every professional wants to be treated with respect. It's what makes an office run smoothly. If you find that your manager is crossing the line and putting you down, address the situation promptly. Here are some things you can say to get the relationship back on a collegial level—or at least to stop offensive behavior. If you have any doubts or concerns at all, or if a situation is egregious or ongoing, consult HR or your legal department.

→ You seem to be too angry to discuss this now. I'll come back later.

→ I prefer that you not raise your voice to me. I'll hear and understand better if you treat me like a teammate.

→ Your [behavior] is unacceptable to me. Please [preferred behavior].

→ I need to talk to you privately about what happened yesterday. It bothered me all night.

→ I feel demeaned by that comment. Did you really mean it that way?

→ I expect to be treated as a team member.

→ Your comments are offensive to me. Stop.

→ I am a professional; so are you. Let's deal with this in a professional manner.

→ I didn't expect [behavior]. I thought you'd [behavior expected].

→ It's not necessary to be brutally honest. Merely being honest would do it.

→ This isn't about power or position. It's about professionalism and respect.

Perfect Phrases to Address Inappropriate Manager Behavior

Some behaviors between employer and employee cross the line. You must address them or they will create a wedge in your business relationships and ultimately damage productivity and morale. At the very least, they make going to work a chore when it should be a pleasure. Consult HR or your legal department if you're unsure of how to address an issue or if the behavior is at all extreme.

→ [Behavior] makes me uncomfortable. Please stop.

→ [Behavior] is unprofessional, and I want our relationship to be strictly professional. Don't [behavior].

→ I'd like to [do what was requested], but it's against company policy.

→ I don't feel comfortable [doing what was requested]. I know you wouldn't want me to do anything that could get us both in trouble.

→ You're standing too close. Can you move back?

→ Sorry, I don't mix business and personal. I'm here to work—and just that, work.

→ Your [e.g., sexual jokes] offend me. They don't belong in the office.

→ This is the third time I've asked you to [stop a behavior]. I've documented it each time. Next time, I will take action by [action].

→ When you [behavior], it keeps me from doing my job. I'm asking you in front of witnesses to stop.

→ What you're doing is inappropriate. Stop it.

→ (For consistent inappropriate actions) I'd hate to report this [behavior] to HR. Stop [behavior] or that will be my next option.

→ This is creating a hostile working environment for me. I am asking you to stop [behavior].

Perfect Phrases to Respond to Unethical Requests

Admins can no longer plead ignorance or coercion when caught doing unethical things for their managers. You can be fired, go to jail, or harm your reputation if you don't stand up for your moral rights. Some ethical violations, such as reproducing copyrighted material, are unlikely to land you in jail but can have a shady feel. Here are phrases for handling major and minor unethical requests unapologetically but also without being self-righteous. Be sure to consult your human resources department if ethical concerns are egregious or persistent.

→ That's against company policy, not to mention the law. You don't want me to do that.

→ I wouldn't feel comfortable doing that.

→ This could put me in jail. No way, nohow.

→ There are some problems with this expense report. You can correct the errors or submit it yourself.

→ This could get us both into trouble. I can't [request].

→ I won't lie. I can say [ethical alternative].

→ My personal ethics are screaming "no."

→ I know you'd never ask me to compromise my ethics. Surely, you didn't mean what I thought I heard you say.

→ I'll do anything within my job description for you, but I won't [lie/steal/mislead].

→ A lot of people do that, but it doesn't feel ethical to me.

→ I understand that saying that isn't lying, but it is misleading. I'm not comfortable with that.

→ I don't lie or deliberately mislead. Give me another option that doesn't ask me to compromise myself.

Perfect Phrases to Respond to Unethical Behavior

Seeing unethical behavior and doing nothing makes you a complacent participant. Here are some phrases for responding to unethical behavior in a way that keeps your ethics and professionalism intact. Avoid self-righteousness or being apologetic about addressing these issues. Again, consult your human resources department if you're unsure of how to respond.

→ I noticed an error in this [report/communication]. Want me to fix it before it goes out?

→ I am responsible for submitting an accurate report. I can't submit this as is.

→ If I thought someone were stealing from the company, I'd be obligated to report it. I know you'd agree.

→ Something isn't quite right. Should we go over the figures again? My records show different numbers.

→ I worry that if you do that, you'll be putting your reputation at risk. Please reconsider.

→ This isn't like you. What's happening? Can I help?

→ There's a better way to do this that doesn't flirt with dishonesty.

Perfect Phrases to Deal with Your Manager's Family and Personal Requests

The bane of admins has always been the clause in the job description that reads, "and all other duties as assigned." You want to be supportive, but what about those totally personal requests that interfere with your company-related tasks? Is it appropriate for you to get presents for your manager's spouse or do research for his or her son's term paper? How about hand-addressing his or her Christmas cards or babysitting when a child is ill? How can you corral those over-and-above requests that take you away from your true job and hinder your productivity?

→ I know this is a personal request. Do you want it to supersede my work assignments?

→ I'd be glad to help out, but right now I am swamped. Would you like the name of a person who freelances these kinds of activities? She could get right on it.

→ I'm not the best person for this job. Here's a better option.

→ (To the family member) I'm sorry, but I can take on delegations only from [name]. You'll have to arrange this with her.

→ I can see why you'd want help with [the activity]. I wish I had the time to give to completing it. Sorry.

→ Is this an overtime activity for me? I could work on it after hours. I'm overloaded with [activity] right now.

→ Please run this by [name]. I have to make sure we can work it into our schedule.

→ I could see if anyone in the department is free to tackle this. I can't take it on with my schedule as it is.

→ I know that my doing personal work for you frees you up for higher company priorities, and I'd like to help. But it's not part of my job description or how I'm evaluated. I don't feel comfortable doing things that aren't company-related.

Perfect Phrases to Deal with Inappropriate Personal Requests from Your Exec

You work for your executive and for your company. If your executive uses you as a personal assistant, it could cheat your company. Then again, it could be that by honoring personal requests, you free up your exec to do more important work. The line isn't black-and-white, but it needs to be drawn somewhere. Also, some of the things your exec wants may not be befitting of your professionalism. You may or may not feel good about taking your manager's car through the car wash. How about lying to his or her spouse about your manager's whereabouts? These phrases will help you define and draw the line.

→ I'll do it this time, but could you make other arrangements in the future? I don't want to get myself in trouble.

→ I'm torn. I want to help you, but I expect [higher exec] wouldn't care for my spending my time that way. Can we check with her?

→ I'm not comfortable doing that. I want to support you, but that compromises my professionalism.

→ If we can get that kind of request into my job description, I'll be happy to do it.

→ That's a personal request that interferes with the job I was hired to do. I'd like to help, but I need to prioritize my company responsibilities.

→ If [higher exec] found out I was [request], I don't think it would bode well for either of us.

Perfect Phrases to Address Requests Outside the Scope of Your Job Description

While you need to be a team player and jump in when help is needed, you don't serve anyone when you drop the ball on your responsibilities because you're overloaded with activities that are not officially a part of your job. If you miss deadlines because you troubleshoot the copy machine or edit reports for another admin, use these phrases to refocus on your true priorities.

➔ I hate the phrase "that's not my job," because it doesn't sound like the response of a team player. But the fact is, if I do that, it will interfere with my ability to do what *is* my job.

➔ I'll do it this time. If it comes up a lot, I'd like to talk about my job description, to keep what I do in alignment with it.

➔ Does this come under "other duties as assigned"? I'd be fine with that except that if I take it on, it would interfere with my official responsibilities. What I can do is [alternative].

➔ That's outside my scope. However, what I can do is [alternative].

Perfect Phrases to Balance Loyalties to Company, Manager, and Others (Including Clients and Board)

Factions don't serve the company well. Admins walk a narrow line of loyalty. Here are some suggestions for how to stay in balance and show you're both understanding and committed to your exec and your company.

➔ Please don't tell me anything you don't want me to share with my manager. That puts me in an unfair and awkward position.

➔ When I share this with staff, I know I'll get questioned about [concerns]. Can we anticipate the questions now so I can respond intelligently?

→ I like your idea. The staff may wonder about [anticipated objections]. How can we address those concerns before they raise them?

→ (To manager) I support you *and* the company. Please don't put me in a position of having to choose between those loyalties.

→ You know I serve two masters. How can I keep you both happy?

→ I'd be glad to do that. Let me just check with [name] to make sure there's nothing else planned for me.

→ No way I'm getting caught in the middle. I'll sit this one out.

→ I'll let [name] speak for herself on this one.

→ I'm hearing some things in the trenches I think you should know. I'd like to give you a heads-up, but I also want to respect confidences so people know it's safe to talk to me. Will you trust me to strike the balance?

Perfect Phrases to Sidestep Being in the Middle of Rumors, Gossip, and Conflict

No one trusts someone who gossips and spreads rumors. Next time someone tries to pull you into negative thinking, ain't-it-awful-ing, and bad-mouthing, here's how to respond and maintain your professionalism.

→ I like working here, and I want to keep it that way. Please don't try to draw me into [criticism/gossip/rumors].

➜ I'm not getting involved in this. I know a setup when I see one.

➜ This kind of conversation drains my energy. I prefer to talk about solutions.

➜ I've learned that gossip and rumors only hurt relationships. Let's talk about something else.

➜ I don't see things the same way as you, and I don't think the discussion is productive.

➜ Lalalalalalala (fingers over ears).

➜ Let's give [name of person being discussed] some credit here. Tearing each other down doesn't serve anything. How can we turn this conversation toward solution?

➜ Engaging in this kind of speculation won't lead to anything good. Let's not go there.

➜ Years ago, I vowed never to spread rumors. I honor that vow.

➜ Let's give him the benefit of a doubt. I don't feel right listening to this. It's all rumors.

Perfect Phrases to Deal Compassionately with Employee Personal Tragedies

The workplace is a microcommunity. We share in each other's triumphs and tragedies. Here are some responses when addressing a colleague's personal tragedy to show you're empathetic, supportive, and caring. (Of course, it helps to find the words if you really do care.)

- → I'll be glad to pick up the slack while you're out, by [action].
- → I'm so sorry for [loss]. Know that I'm here for you.
- → I know you're not at full capacity now. There are some things that need to happen, and I'd like to know what you can handle and what we need to cover.
- → No one expects you to be chipper or running at full steam with what you're dealing with. Can you work with us to make sure your responsibilities are covered while you go through this?
- → I don't know if you want to talk about it or not. I'm here if you do.
- → I don't know what to say except I'm here for you.
- → I'm so very sorry. I can only imagine what you're experiencing.
- → My heart goes out to you.
- → I hated to hear the news. We're all thinking of you here at work.

Perfect Phrases to Manage, Defuse, and Resolve Conflict

Conflict is inevitable. Healthy environments don't dismiss conflict; they address it, learn from it, and build on it. Admins and office pros often see the varying pressures and needs behind complaints and conflict, which puts them in an ideal position to address the situation and move people toward resolution.

→ (To manager) There is conflict in the trenches that we need to address. If we don't, it will affect our productivity.

→ (To manager) We've got to get people back on the same team. We've lost sight of our mission here. Let's find out where we lost our inspiration and what we need to do to get it back.

→ (To manager) People think you have an office pet. That hurts morale. We need to know you've got everyone's back, not a favored few.

→ I don't think they're out to get you here. I think they have pressures you're not aware of, and if you could work with them, you'd find them more willing to work with you on this.

→ I hear your complaint. I'd like to hear what you want and a proposed solution that doesn't make other people out as the bad guys and require them to do all the changing.

→ OK . . . let's look at our end goals. What will get us there and leave our self-respect intact?

→ We can create any kind of office culture we want. Is this dynamic of [pettiness/bickering/gossip] what we want?

→ This isn't a right-or-wrong situation. Pointing fingers like this polarizes us, and that doesn't help a thing. Let's talk without building cases against each other.

→ I'm on your team here. If I've done anything that suggests that I'm not, let me know.

CHAPTER 7

Perfect Phrases to Optimize Work-Flow Procedures

We have multiple pairs of shoes, but we both mainly wear the same ones over and over. Why? They're comfortable and we don't have to give any thought to our choices. We reach for the same old shoes out of habit.

People do much the same thing on the job, with routines. We get something that works and keep using it, well beyond its value or timeliness. Take some of the tasks you perform frequently. Do you ever stop and ask yourself, does anyone read this report? What would happen if I didn't send it to everyone, but waited to see if anyone missed it? Likewise, what about writing up minutes for project meetings, photocopying them for all the participants, putting them in a new binder each time (with indexes, of course), bundling up the ones that need to go UPS, and distributing the rest in-house? Would it make more sense to put the minutes online for everyone to see and access as needed?

Admins are the experts of processes and procedures, especially the ones that cross their desks. Admins and office pros know what it takes to get a job done, and admins can estimate a turnaround time based on other assignments and priorities. It makes sense that you, as the admin, question ineffective procedures and suggest better ways to get better results. Doing so also gives you more control over your schedule and lets you spend time where it is needed most.

This chapter gives you the perfect phrases for getting coworkers (and execs) out of their ho-hum, that's-the-way-it's-always-been-done comfort zone and into more productive ways of doing things. You'll find words for offering new ideas and for getting buy-in on effective protocols, tips for dealing with people who want to jump ahead in the work queue, and techniques to get folks on board and on time.

Perfect Phrases to Get Support for Developing Standard Operating Procedures

The current office situation requires a balance of flexibility and procedure. While there are times to flex, efficiency requires some standard to flex from. Making everything up as you go along is a formula for chaos. These phrases will help you get support for developing workable procedures.

→ It would be much more efficient if we had a standard procedure for [function].

→ I know that a lot of people resist procedures because they're afraid it will limit them. But the right procedure will clear up confusion. For example, [proposed standardized procedure].

→ If all our departments used the same procedure to [process], it would save us time when we interface.

→ I'll start defining standard operating procedures that we can review and develop together so that we're doing things not my way or your way or their way, but our way.

Perfect Phrases to Identify Obstructive, Counterproductive Procedures

Some procedures seem almost prehistoric. Here are some ways to identify and address procedures that don't work.

→ I know we've always done [process] this way. I think there's a better way.

→ I didn't send out the notes, to see if anyone missed them. No one did. I suggest we stop doing that.

→ The other day, [story of what happened due to an outdated procedure]. I suggest we evaluate whether that procedure helps or gets in the way.

→ I notice you didn't follow our procedure on that. Is that because there's a problem with the procedure? Do you think it needs changing?

→ [Another department] handles this in a way that works really well. They [new way]. I'd like us to try that.

→ I asked my colleagues for best practices. Here's what they suggested about [procedure].

→ I did some online searches for ways to handle [procedure]. Here's what came up as the latest trend.

Perfect Phrases to Suggest Changes for Existing Standard Operating Procedures

Leaders don't just point out what's wrong—they suggest better alternatives. Here are phrases to help you take the lead with operating procedures.

→ I suggest that we modify [procedure] by [recommendation].

→ I found a more efficient way to [process]. I suggest we change our method.

→ I'm thinking we do [process] this way out of habit. It would take a little while to start [new way], but once we got used to it, it would save a lot of time.

→ With your permission, I'd like to [change] for a month and see if it makes less work for us with the same or a better result.

→ I went through the procedures manual and updated some of the ones that were out of date. If you agree with my changes, I'll redo the manual and send out the latest copy to everyone.

→ I think it's a good idea to look at the procedures manual once a year and make changes as needed. I'll be glad to take the first attempt at adding, deleting, and changing processes so they work better for us and the folks we interact with.

Perfect Phrases to Get Buy-In for New Procedures and Procedure Changes

Buy-in can make the difference between the success or failure of a procedure. Here are some phrases to get people on board.

→ If we changed the procedure to [change], it would make your job easier by [advantage].

→ What would make you like a new procedure for [process]?

→ I know you're so busy that you're wary of a new way of doing [process]. In the long run it would save you time by [benefit].

→ I understand why you may not want to change the procedure. I felt that way at first. Then I found that [discovery].

➜ I did this [process] two different ways—the old way we always did it and a new way. The new way worked better for me. Take a look.

➜ You know how we keep getting more and more work? Well, I figured out how we could shave off hours by doing [process] a new way.

➜ I'd like to apply my personal wardrobe philosophy to procedures—if we add something, we toss something old.

Perfect Phrases to Simplify Systems and Procedures for Clarity

Some procedures are more complicated than they need to be. Here's how you invite simplification. Note: don't just suggest *that* you simplify. Suggest how.

➜ We get hung up on this procedure. Let's change it to [new procedure wording].

➜ With so few of us here to get the work done, if we changed [old process] to [new process], we could save time and trouble.

➜ Since I will be supporting [number] managers, I suggest we change [old process] to [new process]. If we don't, it will get us at crunch time.

➜ I called a colleague who is a real ace as far as scheduling work flow goes, and she suggested that we try what works in her company. No sense reinventing the wheel.

→ I'll tell you what: let's try it my way for two weeks, and if it isn't better, faster, and simpler, we'll change back to the old way.

Perfect Phrases to Communicate Protocol for Work Requests and Assignments

It's one thing to establish procedures. It's another to get buy-in and anther thing again to break old habits in favor of new protocol. These phrases will help.

→ Please sign in your project on my work schedule. That's so I can keep track of deadlines, priorities, and dates the work came to me.

→ I posted my work schedule so everyone can see what I'm working on and where your request is in the lineup.

→ This is the final work protocol. It incorporates all the managers' suggestions and my input from all our experience.

→ It takes getting used to, but here's how we log in projects now.

→ I put your work request into the format so you can see how the info needs to be formatted.

→ I really need your help in establishing my new project sign-in procedure.

→ It's a simple step. I'll help you get used to it.

→ It takes time for everyone to get the hang of the new system. I think if people saw you using it, it would help motivate them.

→ It's a habit to do it the old way, so how about I remind you each time until you're used to the new way?

→ I saw you didn't sign in your project. You didn't think I'd let you get away with breaking procedure, did you? (ha-ha)

→ Notice I have stars by the names of all the managers who use the new system. When everyone gets a star, I'll spring for doughnuts for the whole group.

Perfect Phrases to Establish Administrative Deadlines

Too many managers figure the deadline to be ten minutes before a project is due, forgetting that it takes time for admins and office pros to put final touches on the work. Get managers used to the phrase "administrative deadline." That term for blocking adequate time, before the final deadline, to allow for your role in project management makes it a concrete reality.

→ Remember to set an administrative deadline for [project].

→ When you meet with [project manager], please remind her to set an administrative deadline so the office staff has time to do our part.

→ My turnaround time for [project] is [time span]. That means in order for you to have it back by [date/time], your part will need to be ready by [date/time].

→ Sit down here a minute so I can show you why [process] takes so much time. From the outside it looks easy. Here's the inside story. That will help you understand why we need administrative deadlines factored into our projects.

→ If the drop-dead deadline for this is [date], the administrative deadline needs to be [earlier date]. And it needs to be admin-ready by then.

Perfect Phrases to Address Procedure Violations

If you let procedures slide, you soon won't have any. No need to get huffy or to be apologetic. Simply use these phrases to address the action when someone tries to bypass a procedure.

→ I know it seems as if you ought to be able to just hand this to me. Here's why the process is important.

→ I don't want to Mommy (or Daddy) you here, but here's how we do this. Group procedure, not mine.

→ I'd be happy to do that for you once you've [procedure].

→ I don't like procedures that take extra time any more than you do, but the reason why we have this one is that [reason].

→ If you were my only manager, I'd let it (the lapse in procedure) slide. Since I support other managers too, I need for you to [procedure].

→ If you do [process], I can meet your deadline by [time] today. Otherwise, it won't be completed until late tomorrow.

Perfect Phrases to Establish Priorities for Reporting to Multiple Managers

If you report to multiple managers who all think they should be your first priority, you will go home very tired at the end of the day. These phrases will help you establish priorities when you support a group.

➜ Because there are so many of you, I need to stick to procedures.

➜ The way I prioritize my assignments is by [criteria—e.g., urgency/first-come-first-served/position of the originator]. That means this assignment will get done [when].

➜ I need all my managers to get together and decide how I prioritize assignments. I need clear guidelines you've all agreed to, and I need to be left out of any disagreements if you change the rules.

➜ (To group) I suggest I prioritize your assignments by [criteria]. I'd like for you to offer your ideas and for us to agree on how we'll prioritize and then honor that agreement.

➜ My job description says my priority is to [item]. That's how I am evaluated, so I take that to be the best measure of a job well done. Unless that changes, that's my criterion for how I manage your projects.

➜ As much as I'd like to [sidestep the policy], we've all agreed to [process]. If this doesn't work for you, bring it up for discussion at the next departmental meeting.

CHAPTER 8

Perfect Phrases to Make Requests and Negotiate

They say, "Ask and you shall receive." It's not always true, but asking sure helps! As it did when Susan orchestrated the writing of a six-hundred-page (!) collaborative book and her name was left off the draft cover. Hello! It turned out all she had to do was ask. The reply? "Oh, I'm sorry. We can list you as General Editor." Too easy!

How many times have you needed a certain piece of equipment or office supply and, seeing it wasn't there, assumed you wouldn't get it and worked around it, knowing your life would be easier if you had it? What about assignments? Have you ever struggled through something that someone delegated to you, when you knew there was a real expert down the hall who could whip it out in an hour? Have you ever been so bogged down that you went home in tears at night because you could never leave with a clean desk . . . yet never asked for help? How many times have you gone into a performance review expecting to hear how wonderful you are and what a nice raise you'll be receiving in your next paycheck, only to hear what you could be doing better and that your salary is capped because you're at the top of your scale?

Asking for what you want can take courage, but developing good negotiation skills provides that courage. If you do your homework, if you bolster your claim with substantial facts, if you provide your information early on and allow time for your request to be digested, you very likely will get what you want, need, and deserve. It's all in the asking . . . and this chapter will be your guide.

Perfect Phrases to Negotiate with Vendors

If you order supplies, you really are managing or at least helping to manage the office budget. The decisions you make and the prices you negotiate impact the success of your department and organization. These phrases will help you ask for a better deal.

→ I have some comparative figures with me from [other vendors/similar positions/online suppliers]. What can we do to match these numbers?

→ I had another amount in mind. This is [higher/lower] than I expected.

→ We can seal the deal right now if you [proposal].

→ There have been some changes in the [department/budget/specs]. We'll need to adapt the [e.g., lease/discount] accordingly.

→ I value [your business/working with you]. Let's put our heads together and make this work—for both of us!

→ You can do better than that. What can you offer me?

→ I'm disappointed with this amount. Can we [talk again/renegotiate] in six months?

→ I know you wouldn't want to lose the account over [amount]. Is that really the best you can do?

→ I don't want to walk away from this. What's the very best deal you can give me?

→ If you can give me [amount/concession], I have the authority to sign right now.

→ Let's both give a little on this and meet in the middle.

→ What is the best you can do?

Perfect Phrases to Negotiate Assignments

Assignments are often negotiable. While you don't want to come across as not being a team player, it doesn't hurt to tailor assignments to your interests and aspirations. It always makes sense to negotiate assignments that are in conflict with other obligations or that are so far outside of your skill sets as to be counterproductive for you to take on.

→ What would you think if I started [project]?

→ I'm interested in developing [skill]. I'd like to take on [project].

→ Is there any way we can get me some help on [project]? I'd like to take on the assignment, but I'm concerned that it will interfere with my other projects.

→ I have ideas about creative ways we can get help with this so it won't interfere with my other obligations.

→ What part of my existing workload can we delegate or drop to free up my time to take this project on?

→ I can get that done if [necessary condition(s)].

→ I'm good at [task], while [name] is great at [other task]. Is it a problem if we trade areas of expertise for these two projects?

→ If I do [subproject], can the full project wait until [date]? I know you need [parts] soon, but if I can divide it up like that, other priorities won't suffer.

Perfect Phrases to Ask for General Help and Assistance

We office professionals pride ourselves on competence. By the same token, we can neglect to ask for help when we need it. Here are some perfect phrases for you to get the help you need without appearing incompetent.

→ I'm juggling a lot of high priorities right now. Do you have time to help me today?

→ I need your expertise to get it all done today. Could you [request]?

→ I'm in over my head today. Could you help me on a couple of things?

→ I'm coming to you because you're the fastest worker I know. I need [specific need] by [time]. Could you give me a hand?

→ It's hard for me to ask for help, but today I'm doing it!

→ I'm being humbled by all the work on my plate today. Can you help?

→ You have always said you've got my back. I sure need you today!

→ You can help me greatly by giving me another day on this assignment. Will you do that?

→ I'm a can-do kind of gal (or guy), but that means knowing when I can't do it, and today I need help.

→ I may be wonder woman (or superman), but today I need help.

→ I want to do a superlative, amazing job on this assignment. To do that, I need help with [request].

→ I'm good, but I'm not that good. I need help with [request].

→ I left my cape at home today and need some help.

→ I know sometimes I'm afraid that if I help someone with something, it will become my job. I'm buried today and wonder if you can [task] for me. I promise I won't make a habit of asking.

→ I don't like asking other people to help me do my job, but today I'm asking.

Perfect Phrases to Ask for Tech Help

Even if you're used to technology, there are times when you will need technical support. Here are some ways you can be prepared to geek-speak and get things back up and running—without alienating tech support.

→ I've tried [A, B, and C], and that didn't solve the problem. What should I do now?

→ This happened twice before. I've documented what I was doing and the exact error message that came up on the screen. Can you shed some light on this?

→ Here's what I'm trying to do. How can I get there?

→ I'm a beginner in [e.g., pivot tables]. Can you explain them in words even a rookie like me can understand?

→ We pooled all our questions and problems and concerns so you'll have to make just one trip to the department. We're ready for you.

→ I checked with the other admins, and they didn't know the answer either. I'll teach the other admins what I learn from you.

→ I'm not following you. Would you watch me while I try that maneuver the way I understand you to be saying?

→ I'll remember this better if you slow down. I'm having trouble following your keystrokes, and I want to get this down pat so I don't have to ask you again.

Perfect Phrases to Ask for Additional Office Help

Most companies respond to tough economic times by cutting back on staff—even when the workload hasn't diminished accordingly. That means that many people take on additional responsibilities to pick up the slack. While this works in the short run, it takes its toll on morale, productivity, and employee health. When it's time to ask for additional support, phrase your comment in a way that will get you what you want and what you need. Here are some examples.

→ This pace isn't sustainable. We're burning out and becoming less efficient. We need help.

→ We're like the juggler who can juggle so many balls and no more. Add one more and we risk dropping them all.

→ If we could do a good job of this without extra help, we would. We can't, and the cost of not getting the help we need is poor quality and low morale.

→ I'm acutely aware of the need to keep staff costs down. I also know how important this project is to the bottom line, and we need help.

→ We're so efficient, we may seem like machines, but we're not. We need help.

→ I can do this alone but not well.

→ I've calculated department overtime. It's less expensive to bring in a temp.

→ We need extra help to meet the new deadlines. Here are some ideas for [adding a part-time worker for this project]. [Temp agency] has people with the experience we need, and the cost won't put us over budget.

→ I can get a top student in here next week as an unpaid intern if we [e.g., provide a mentor or supervisor]. We need the help. Are you open to that?

→ I've figured out an exchange with the admins in [department] to get us through the crunch, if we'll help them when they need extra help later this fall. Does that work for you?

Perfect Phrases to Request Technology Upgrades

Technology is a tool of your trade. As a professional, you need the right tools to do your job well. Ask for the upgrades you need.

→ The [current technology] is a bit like using an eight-track player. We need an upgrade.

→ I can keep using [technology], but it limits me by [limit].

→ [Technology] will save us time and money over the course of [time span]. Here are the figures.

→ I looked at the latest technology on the market, and it appears that if I had [specific technology], it would pay for itself within a year.

→ IT tells me [specific technology] will help us do the job cheaper, faster, and better. Here's why.

→ I talked to a colleague who really knows her stuff about our bottlenecks. She said they got around that problem by upgrading to [technology]. Shall we give it a try here?

Perfect Phrases to Ask for Office Equipment

Asking for equipment is like asking for technology. A cost-benefit analysis can help.

→ This will help my productivity by [benefit].

→ This will help you by [benefit].

→ Our [equipment] is inadequate because [issue]. I've researched a solution and discovered [solution].

→ If we got a [equipment], I see five ways we can use it. [Ways.]

→ [Equipment] will save us [number] hours over [time span], which translates into [total amount it costs to pay employees for those hours].

→ I've highlighted all the new features in [technology] that will allow us to do more with fewer people. I've checked—we haven't used all our equipment money this year. Can I get your approval to order it?

Perfect Phrases to Request Reasonable Accommodation

If you have a disability, it is very reasonable to request reasonable accommodation. Even though the law requires your employer to provide reasonable accommodation, specifics involve negotiation. You want your employer to work with you, and you, in turn, will work with your employer. Get HR involved if you're unsure of what you're entitled to or what will be most effective.

→ I can do this job with the accommodation of [request].

→ I have a few requirements that are unique to my situation. If you can accommodate me by [request], I'll be able to do a first-rate job.

→ Because of [handicap], having [accommodation] will help me roll out the work faster.

→ While I don't mind [status quo], if I had [accommodation], I think my work quality would greatly increase.

→ Everyone does things differently. I need [accommodation] to do my best.

Perfect Phrases to Ask for a Raise

While a rare manager may notice what an outstanding job you're doing and offer a raise, more often than not, you need to ask and negotiate. You'll find phrases here and more phrases to negotiate for a higher salary in Chapter 15, Perfect Phrases for Career Management.

→ I'd like to talk about my salary targets for this year to make sure we're on the same page and to make sure my performance is in line.

→ I'd like to meet with you to discuss my salary. What time works for you?

→ My responsibilities have outpaced my salary. Let's talk.

→ I've documented my contributions to our bottom line and where I've saved and made money for the company. I know I don't just need to show you why I deserve more—I need to help you convince the board.

→ In the past six months I've saved the company [amount] by [action].

→ In the past six months I've made the company [amount] by [action].

→ I'm in an excellent position to bring in money by [intention]. That easily translates into [amount] in a raise, as I see it.

Perfect Phrases to Ask to Be Sent to Conferences and Receive Training

Include professional development in your list of things you negotiate for.

→ We have [problem]. This workshop will give me some solutions.

→ I highlighted the benefits to the department of my attending this workshop. Will you sign your approval?

→ In my last performance review, we discussed [skills needed]. I've been looking for a good, low-cost training session on this and found one that's perfect for me.

→ I looked at ways to shorten the turnaround time for [task]. Here's a workshop on [technology] that will help that happen.

→ I'd like to attend this workshop. It will [benefits]. I'll teach the other admins what I've learned after I return.

→ Part of the departmental plan is to [mandate]. This conference will give me the skills I need to [related function].

→ Here are ten reasons I need to attend this session. Here are ten reasons for you to want me to go.

CHAPTER 9

Perfect Phrases to Clarify Job Expectations

I often ask audience members how many of them should get extra points at work if they can guess what their job is. I get a laugh every time—and a roomful of hands. I also ask how many discovered what their job was at the performance review, when they were rated poorly for something they didn't know was a part of their job. I always get hands up on that one too. Susan knows an admin who thought she was doing an excellent job by doing what she had done before—organizing and supporting others. She was shocked to learn she wasn't meeting standards. Her new position required innovation and revenue production.

There's one more question I ask my audience members—how many have a job description that reflects what they actually do? I don't get many hands on that one.

A hard part of any job, be it in a new company, in a new department, or just a new assignment, is to figure out what you're expected to do and how. That's why it is essential to clarify guidelines up front. You don't want to guess and risk guessing wrong.

Part of being an office professional is defining your own parameters. Teamwork in the workplace means everyone is a contributor. Admins no longer "just" do other people's work. They have their own expertise and dominion. That means that to do your job well, you need clearly defined, agreed-upon, and understood job expectations.

It's like setting the rules of any sport before you play. In a smoothly functioning football team, for example, all the players know what the role of a guard is and don't expect guards to indiscriminately fill the role of quarterback. If the team forgets what the guard is there for and skilled at doing, it's the guard's job to clarify it.

So, whether your job is new or evolves over time, here are some perfect phrases that will help you clarify the scope of responsibilities for which you'll be held accountable and how you'll be evaluated.

Perfect Phrases to Differentiate Between Job Standards and Goals

Job standards are requirements for anyone in a position. Job goals are elective and exist to inspire growth and stretching. Standards are absolutes. Goals are optional. Don't strive to achieve goals at the expense of standards. You don't want your manager to assume your goals are standards and to evaluate your performance at a lower level because you aimed high and missed.

→ I'd like to go over my targets here and make sure I know which are standards and which are goals.

→ By my next performance review, I plan to be able to [goal]. I set that goal to stretch my ability beyond the usual job standards.

→ My understanding is that [standard] is a standard and [goal] is a goal. Is my understanding correct?

→ I've separated out my job standards and my goals so I don't sacrifice the standards, which are priorities, for my own goals.

→ I set my goals high to stretch myself. I could set an easy goal that I know I can reach. I tell you that so that if I fall short, I won't be penalized for aiming so high. Make sense?

Perfect Phrases to Clarify Job Description Content

You and your manager may not have the same idea of what your job is. Don't assume, and don't guess. Clarify—before you get a bad review for not meeting expectations you weren't aware of.

➜ The job description says I [responsibility—e.g., respond to inquiries about delivery times]. I want to make sure I have the same understanding of what that means that you do. Does that mean that when [event—e.g., someone doesn't get a shipment], I should [action—e.g., handle it myself without consulting you]?

➜ I find some of the definitions in my job description a bit abstract. Can we go over each point in terms of what it would look like in an ordinary day?

➜ I'd rather confirm now that I correctly understand how you view my job description and make sure we're on the same page. Could you give me a mock performance review soon so I can see how my interpretation and performance match your expectations?

➜ I want to be the best office manager you've ever had. How would you describe an office-pro-from-heaven to your colleagues?

Perfect Phrases to Prioritize Job Activities

If you're doing a great job of something your manager doesn't care about, it won't help anyone. Make sure your manager's priorities are your priorities. If your manager's priorities for you seem off target, don't just insist on doing what you think matters. Have a collaborative discussion to set mutual priorities.

→ My job description lists [responsibility] first, but I want to make sure it is my first priority. If you were to put these responsibilities in order according to how important they are to you, how would you structure the list?

→ If everything is a priority, nothing is. That's why I want us to decide priorities, even though everything is important.

→ What do you see as the most important thing I do?

→ I get the impression that you see [responsibility] as my top priority. I can see why that would be true from where you sit. From my vantage point I see [other responsibility] as a greater priority. Can I tell you why?

→ I'd like to do [project] because [reason]. If I do, it would interfere with [other project]. Do I have your approval to prioritize that way?

→ I like to put first things first. Where I see the beginning point is [priority].

Perfect Phrases to Align Your Job Priorities with Evaluation Procedures

Evaluations often do not reflect the actual requirements of the job. If that's the case for you, see if you can get the criteria adapted. It's frustrating to do a superior job on true priorities and get rated based on incidental, insignificant criteria.

→ I need your help. I'm spending a lot of time doing [area], and while it's important, it isn't part of my evaluation. Plus, it takes time away from projects that are. How can we fix that?

→ I'd like to update my job description. My responsibilities have changed, but my description hasn't. That means I can be doing what you need me to do and still get penalized at the review.

→ It's good to begin with the end in mind. I'd like to look ahead to my next performance review and look at what I need to do to get an excellent one. Can you help?

→ We're redefining my job description. I want to make sure that's reflected in my evaluation. Will you help?

Perfect Phrases to Address Job Obstacles

Sometimes outside obstacles make it impossible for you to meet expectations. The trick is to get help and support without sounding as if you're whining and complaining.

→ My job description calls for me to [activity], but there are things that interfere with my being able to do my job that I don't control. I need your help.

→ I want to do a great job. I need your help with [obstacle] to do that.

→ I don't want to sound as if I'm complaining, because I'm not. I'm looking for a solution. There are obstacles I can't control that keep me from doing my job. Can we brainstorm ways to solve this?

→ I honestly think anyone in my position would have a difficult time getting the job done, because of external factors. I give it my all, but I need help with some obstacles so I'm not set up to fail.

→ My job includes responsibility for [responsibility] but doesn't give the authority to get it done. What do you recommend?

→ I'd like to discuss the obstacles I face in getting my job done and the remedies I can think of. Will you collaborate with me to fix this?

Perfect Phrases to Finesse Your Job Description

We aren't fans of inflated job descriptions, but the fact is that office pros often have job descriptions that don't fairly reflect the professionalism and skill it takes to do the job right. Play with your description a bit. Even if you can't get your finessed definitions into the formal document, use terms that honor what you do when you talk about your job.

→ My job description says I write memos. It is more accurate to say I compose them. I craft them with care for clarity and effectiveness.

→ I composed a memo about [topic] so we will get the answers we need.

→ My job description says I sort the mail. But actually, I answer correspondence for certain managers, pull info to go with some inquiries, and do a lot more than serve as mail carrier. Saying I prioritize communication sums it up better.

→ I prioritized your calls and letters for you so you can respond to the most important ones first.

→ My job description says I order supplies. It's more accurate to say I manage the supply budget and inventory. I purchase all supplies and track inventory. I carefully monitor how I apply our resources.

→ My job description says I handle customer complaints. It's more accurate to say I manage customer relations. I don't just try to make the complaints go away—I work to keep our customers for life.

→ I'd like to make these changes in my job description. Here's why.

Perfect Phrases to Enhance Your Job Responsibilities

Has your job gotten too small for you? Are you ready to play for higher stakes? Here are some phrases for you to employ to enhance your responsibilities. (Note: sometimes the best way to expand your role and autonomy is to simply do it. As one admin said to me, "Keep on walking until someone tells you to stop.")

→ There are a few requests I pass on to you that I believe I can handle myself. Would you be OK with it if I did?

→ I'd like to take care of more things without bothering you. If I know I can handle something I'm passing on to you now, how about I just take care of it?

→ I'm interested in developing my ability to [skill]. Are you open to my taking that on?

→ I notice we've been struggling to get a good job done on [project aspect—e.g., design]. I'd like to try my hand at it. It may take a few attempts to get it right, but I'm sure I could learn. Are you open to that?

→ There are some things we're contracting out that I can handle (or learn to handle).

→ I've learned how you operate, and I can represent you at [event/meeting].

CHAPTER 10

Perfect Phrases to Clarify and Manage Assignments

Efficiency is doing the job right. Effectiveness is doing the right job right.

If you find yourself guessing what your manager wants, you're probably not being effective. I occasionally receive calls from admins on their managers' behalf and don't understand what the managers want them to get from me. They ask me to help them figure out why the manager asked them to call me. We guess for a while, and then they go back to the manager for clarification. Sometimes it takes two or three calls before we get it figured out. Clearly, that is not an efficient use of anyone's time. It would have been far more efficient for the manager to call me directly.

It's nice when managers are clear up front. It's nice when managers do things themselves that they can do more efficiently. It's nice when managers consider your workload when they assign projects. It's nice, but it's not your manager's job to manage your workload. It's yours. It's not your manager's job to make sure you understand what he or she wants. It's yours. It's not your manager's job to keep you efficient. It's yours. If you receive unclear instructions or impossible requests, or if you are asked to do things that are better done by someone else, these phrases will help you have the conversations you need in order to manage your assignments.

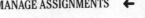

Perfect Phrases to Ask Questions to Clarify Work Assignments

I invite my staff to ask three questions about every request I make of them, even if they don't feel the need. It uncovers questions they didn't know they had. Here are phrases you can use to make sure you understand—even if you think you already do.

→ I think I understand what you're looking for, but to make sure, I'd like to ask some questions.

→ What would a perfect outcome look like?

→ What authority do I have to get [help/answers/support]?

→ I'm thinking my first step on this would be to [step]. Does that sound right?

→ How is this different from [previous assignment]?

→ Are you looking for a finished presentation or raw data?

→ Are you looking for technical input or creative or both?

→ Are there any questions you would ask if you were me now?

→ What kinds of mistakes have people run into doing this that I should avoid?

→ I'm going to risk asking a question that may sound dumb but will keep me from making mistakes.

Perfect Phrases to Say Work Isn't Ready for Admin Input

As is true of everyone else, managers are busy. That means they may turn something over for your processing that they haven't thought through or organized effectively for your input. These phrases will help you get work in just the way you need it so that you can get it done and meet your manager's expectations.

→ This needs more attention. Before I work my magic on it, I need you to work your magic on it by [request].

→ If I work with this before it's right, we'll waste my time and yours. I see some things it needs before I can do my part.

→ I could [fill in gaps/correct errors], but you would still be responsible for any errors in it, even if I make them. I'd like you to complete your [data] before I do my part with it.

→ It would save us both time if you'd take one more look at this before I work with it. Otherwise, I expect we'll be going back and forth for clarification, and that wouldn't be efficient for either of us.

→ You were in a hurry to get this to me, weren't you! Not that it shows or anything! I noticed a few things you missed.

→ We set administrative deadlines to make sure the office staff has enough time to do our parts of it well. I suspect that caused you to rush and miss a few things. How about I give this back to you and we can extend the administrative deadline by a day?

Perfect Phrases to Make Your Work Visible

It's both to admins' credit and detriment that they make things look so easy that people don't realize how skilled they really are. These phrases will help you make your work visible without sounding as if you're bragging, giving too much detail—or complaining.

→ I have my projects posted on the wall there. Here's how your project fits into the big picture.

→ I jumped through a lot of hoops to pull this off for you.

→ I'm so excited about how I [one-sentence update on progress].

→ I want to sit you down to show you what it takes to do what you're asking. I'm glad to do it—I just want you to know what's involved.

→ I had a great day today. I accomplished [achievement].

→ I need a high five for what I accomplished today.

→ I got to use my skills in [skill] today when I [accomplishment].

→ I got a compliment today that reflects nicely on us both. [Praise you received.]

Perfect Phrases to Decline, Adapt, or Defer Assignments

In addition to considering these helpful phrases, review Chapter 7 for more examples of how to negotiate assignments.

→ You know me . . . I'm always ready, willing, and able to jump in when a project needs extra hands. On a long-term basis, I think this project would be a misuse of my skills and would be better done by [alternative].

→ If I do that, I won't be able to do [other assignment]. I think it would be wise for me to pass.

→ While it would be an opportunity for me to do that, it's just not the time for me to take on something of that scale (or other *legitimate* reason).

→ That would require my developing [new skill set]. While I love the idea of learning how, I suggest we [alternative].

→ I could do that if [aspect] were handled by someone else.

→ I can see that this project is dear to your heart. If we do it, I'd like us to do it right. How about if we wait until after [event—e.g., budgets] to start so we can give it the focus it deserves?

→ The project is a great idea. I don't think I'm the right person for the job because [reason].

→ I know this project would help you professionally. I'd like to be a part of that. I also know it would interfere with what I'm doing now.

Perfect Phrases to Get Results Without Authority

There are three kinds of power available to admins and office pros: knowledge power (what you know), people power (who you know), and positional power (authority). If you don't have positional power in a situation, you can rely more on the other two sources.

→ We're in this together, and it will benefit all of us for this to happen. Can I count on your support?

→ Let me call [name's] assistant and see if I can get the ball rolling.

→ I know another way to make this happen.

→ I know this process inside and out. I'll show you how if you help me. Then you'll know how to do it when you need to.

→ Let me get my network involved in this. We're always covering for each other.

→ Can I call in a favor right now? I could use your help.

→ I am aware that you're higher on the org chart than I am, and it may seem odd for me to ask you to do something for me. But as part of the team, can you help me here?

→ I took care of all the details so all you need to do is [request].

Perfect Phrases to Delegate Up

Since you and your manager are part of a team, it can be appropriate for you to delegate work up the ladder to your manager. You probably don't want to call it delegation. These phrases will work better.

→ I can get that done for you if you help me with [request].

→ Although [task—e.g., answering the phones] is way below your pay grade, could you cover for me so I can get [project] done?

→ I'd be happy to [task] for you. However, since you made the initial contacts, I suspect if I do, I won't be able to answer all the questions. I think it would make more sense for you to take this one on.

→ I know [name], and I feel pretty sure we'd be more likely to get a yes if the request came from you.

→ I'd be happy to do that for you. But I think it would be more efficient if you did it, because [reason]. Is there something I can do for you to free your time for this?

→ I can save you time on that by showing you how to do it yourself.

→ May I show you how to find the answer faster than by asking me?

Perfect Phrases to Eliminate Unnecessary Paperwork and Bureaucratic Hurdles

Chances are your procedures are wrought with outdated and unnecessary obstacles. Here's how you can eliminate many hurdles that keep you from getting the job done. For a more complete list, see Chapter 7.

→ I don't think this is the best way for us to be doing this anymore. I suggest that we modify [procedure] by [recommendation].

→ I understand why [e.g., we limited social media use in the beginning]. I really think that's creating a lot of unnecessary barriers for us now. Can I research [e.g., more liberal social media policies that seem to work]?

→ Are we doing [procedure] this way out of habit? It slows the turnaround down a lot. Who would be the best person for me to talk to about getting the process changed or updated?

→ I went through the procedures book and updated some of the ones that were out of date. If you'll take a quick look, I'll redo the manual and send out the latest copy to everyone.

→ Are we legally required to maintain this paperwork? I wonder if we could skip it.

→ There's an informal way people do this that violates procedure but gets the job done. I can't see that it's doing any harm, so I'd like to see how we could make the informal procedure the formal one.

→ What is [type of data] used for? How can we simplify the form so it's not such a drag?

Perfect Phrases to Get a Manager to See You're Stretched Too Far

We've come to recognize that we're not machines. Well . . . most of us have. If your manager hasn't gotten the memo yet, let him or her know that even you have limits.

→ I can sprint for a while, but I've been sprinting for three months on this project. If I don't slow down, I'll collapse before I hit the finish line. That won't serve anyone or anything.

→ I find myself making mistakes I never made before. The reason is obvious. I'm doing too much.

→ The question isn't, will I take on one more thing—it's whether I can. It has reached that point. I think this could be the last straw for me.

→ I used to love my job and working here. My spirit is dampened now—not because of the kind of work, but because of the volume of work.

→ If I say yes to one more thing, I'm concerned that I'll catch what's been going around and not be able to work at all. We really need to calibrate my work so I can have time to recoup between projects.

Perfect Phrases to Communicate the Scope and Challenges of an Assignment

Your manager doesn't always know what a project requires unless you tell him or her. For example, I once asked an assistant to e-mail an invoice, not knowing that it would require purchasing and installing software that we wouldn't use much. Had she explained, I would have found a better alternative. Let your manager know what fulfilling certain requests requires.

→ I can do that for you, but just so you know, there's more involved than meets the eye.

→ I know it looks simple to do that. I can do it, but it won't be simple. Please let me explain what's involved so you can make an informed decision about whether I really should do this.

→ I won't bore you with all the details about what that would involve, but let me give you an overview so you know what it takes, and we can decide if an alternative would make more sense.

→ Can I tell you what I went through last time to make that happen? I'm not looking for pats on the back; I just want you to know what's involved so we can adapt my other responsibilities to pull this off.

CHAPTER 11

Perfect Phrases to Be the Office Innovator

Admins are noted for attention to detail and the ability to create and improve on processes. Alas, many never take the initiative to step up and suggest changes that would save the company time, money, and resources. Why?

Lots of reasons, but a key reason is that admins often don't feel they are true, legitimate members of the work team. They think they are "just admins" and don't have the right or the know-how to operate on par with the other professionals on staff.

How wrong that assumption is! If they could only hear managers talk in training sessions, as we do, they'd hear, "No one ever taught me how to work with or really use an admin when I was getting an M.B.A." "I have no idea what admins do or what they are capable of. I guess I just assign them things that I think an admin would do." Some managers think office professionals are only order takers. Most are finding they are indispensable members of their teams.

Admins today create and give PowerPoint presentations, stand in for their managers at meetings, train others on software applications, troubleshoot technology problems, publish newsletters, maintain websites, employ Twitter and Facebook to reach customers, and coordinate projects with teammates at other stations—down the hall and halfway around the word.

So, whose job is it to liberate you as an office professional to take on new roles and responsibilities, initiate improvements, and help the company keep pace with changes in the administrative field? Yours, of course!

It's up to you to step forward and demonstrate your professionalism and your value to the work team. Your manager won't fully know what you are capable of unless you let him or her know. Plus, while being the one who moves the company into the new era doesn't guarantee job security, it sure doesn't hurt.

Perfect Phrases to Offer Training and Coaching

Everyone knows admins usually are the first adopters and primary users of office software applications. That makes admins the natural go-to people when someone needs help. In fact, admins often are the only ones who know how most things in the office work, which is why admins often offer to train and coach. Here are some phrases to use when you have an opportunity to let others know your worth.

→ Would you like to learn a faster way to do that? I know you're always very busy, and it can save you a few extra minutes each day.

→ How about I take a shot at that and show you another way to do it?

→ This can be frustrating. Don't expect to learn it all in a day.

→ You don't have to be a geek to learn these shortcuts. They're easier than you may think.

→ I've trained all my execs on this application. Would you like a quick lesson?

→ I can save you time on that. Rather than passing it along to me for [function], if you do [action] and [action], you won't need me in the mix. It will speed things up for you.

→ I can answer that for you, but I'd rather show you how to look it up yourself so you won't have to track me down next time. Are you open to that?

→ When you notice me doing something in a less efficient way than possible, I'd like for you to tell me. Would you like me to do the same for you?

→ When I have an idea for you or think you may need help, how would you like me to offer? I don't want to imply that I don't think you know what you're doing.

Perfect Phrases to Train and Coach Gracefully

Managers are less likely to be threatened by having office staff teach and coach them than they once were, but it's still a good idea to tread lightly.

→ I'll write down the steps for you to follow after I show you the tricks of the trade. That should help you when you're on your own.

→ Here's the way I do it. See if it works any better for you. If it doesn't, I need for you to show me what you do.

→ First I'll show you and describe what I do. Then I'll talk you through doing it yourself. After that, I'd like for you to explain to me what you're doing while you do it.

→ I tried to do it that way too. It makes sense, but I found it's quicker to [alternative].

→ It's simple once you get the hang of it, but it can take several attempts to figure out how it all works.

Perfect Phrases to Suggest New Opportunities

Admins and office pros are a source of innovative ideas for their managers. Here are some ways to share your ideas and offer new opportunities.

→ I was thinking we could try [opportunity]. I'll be checking into it and keeping you posted.

→ My buds at the networking meeting said something that I thought could lead to a great opportunity for us. They were telling me [information].

→ I'm wondering why we don't try [idea]. I think market conditions are favorable for it now.

→ Wouldn't it be great if we [idea].

→ It's easy for me to sit here and suggest things we could be doing. I know implementing them is a lot harder. But I'm seeing some things that could be opportunities for us. Want to hear what they are, in case one might strike a chord with you?

→ I have an idea that looks really good from where I sit. Can I run it by you so you can tell me how it looks from where you sit?

→ I have an idea that is lighting my fire. I would need some help from you to make it happen, but it's so exciting to me that I'd like to do most of the legwork on it. Can I share it?

→ Have you considered [idea]?

→ You might have already considered this idea—but in case you haven't, I was thinking [idea].

→ Things are changing fast. I see a lot of people finding [opportunities/customers/strategic partnerships] on [e.g., social media]. I'd like to head up a group to explore how we could [e.g., use social media effectively].

Perfect Phrases to Express Opinions

Your opinion matters. You may see only a part of the picture, but the part you see adds to the total understanding. When you express opinions, do it in ways that will have you taken seriously without sounding overbearing.

→ I'd like to throw my opinion into the mix.

→ I have an opinion on this subject. May I share it?

→ I know the final decision on this is yours. I'd like to offer some input that may or may not influence your decision.

→ I've reviewed the facts and data and formed an opinion here that is different from yours. I'd like to share it, and if my opinion is flawed, I'd like for you to tell me how and why.

→ This is an area I've studied. That's why I have some carefully considered opinions on the topic.

→ Can I weigh in on this?

→ If it were I, [idea].

→ It's not up to me, but if it were, [idea].

→ If I were making this decision, [idea].

→ I have some insights that may be useful to you here.

→ You make some excellent points. I'd like to talk about some things you might not have considered.

→ Have you considered [idea]?

Perfect Phrases to Recommend Initiatives

Who is in a better position to innovate than someone who deals with employees at all levels? Chances are excellent that you see opportunities and possible initiatives every day. When you see possibilities, use these phrases to introduce them.

→ Did you ever consider we could be [initiative]?

→ I heard about an initiative at [another company] that I think could work really well for us. What if we were to [idea]?

→ I'm considering forming a [e.g., Toastmasters group/Masterminds group]. Can I have your blessing on it?

→ I notice people feel [disconnected/isolated/left out of the loop/compartmentalized]. I was thinking we could [initiative] to deal with it.

→ I've been around you long enough to learn how you think, and I have an initiative I think you'll like. What if we were to [idea]?

→ I get to see how things play out in ways that you wouldn't from your position. I notice we get a lot of questions and complaints about [area]. I was thinking we could address that by [idea].

CHAPTER 12

Perfect Phrases to Bring Out the Best in Everyone

Some people naturally bring out the best in others. Some bring out the worst. How's the culture in your workplace? What role do you play in shaping that culture? Is it a consciously positive one?

We're all affected by existing cultures. That doesn't make us cultural victims. If you think creating and shaping the culture is up to leadership, management, and HR, you're dropping the ball. Admins and other office pros are in a unique position of subtle and not-so-subtle power to influence and even transform the office and corporate cultures.

An excellent example is Krista, who decided she would get the admins in her company to talk to each other over brown-bag lunches that did not include management—but ended up getting management to work collaboratively. Another is David, who put an end to much of the gossip in his department by providing access to information that management hadn't realized the staff needed to know.

How do you empower others? How do you bring out the best in others to create a more positive culture? Well—you *don't* do it by criticizing, moralizing, or chastising. You do it by speaking to people's highest natures and painting pictures of possibilities. You also do it by being constructive, uplifting, and positive yourself.

Why you? Again, as an office administrator, you're in a unique position to affect the culture. Admins and office pros are in contact with employees at many levels of an organization. Admins represent their managers, and they can do that in ways that either help or hinder how the managers are perceived. Admins interface interdepartmentally and externally. You see relationship dynamics that others don't. So, don't shake your head and say, "Someone's got to do something." Nod your head and say, "I'm committed to empowering others and improving the office culture." Then use the phrases that work.

Perfect Phrases to Promote Interdepartmental Communication

If you and your colleagues wonder what those "idiots" down the hall or across the globe with whom you interface are smoking, it's time to stop being critical and start being collaborative. Or, worse, if you and your colleagues have forgotten other departments exist at all, it's time to wake up to discover how a little interdepartmental communication can go a very long way. Keep these phrases in your arsenal.

→ I notice our departments aren't talking to each other as well as we could be.

→ We're in separate departments, but we still share the same goals.

→ We need to make sure this will work with [department].

→ We're having a hard time working with your [e.g., marketing plan/software/directives]. How can we all get together to coordinate our separate roles here?

→ We're not getting what we need from your department on [project], and we wonder if there's something about the [format/time line/specs] that isn't working for you here.

→ Since this project crosses departments, let's set up a meeting and discuss who does what by when. That should really streamline the work flow.

→ Can you tell me how you'd like the information for [project] to come to you from our area? I want to make things easy for you.

→ Would you like to spend a day with me, seeing how the projects start from this point? Then I could do the same with you. We'd end up better understanding how what we each do helps or hinders the other.

→ What can I do to make things easier for you and your team?

→ Before you get too far down the line on [project], I recommend you talk to [department], since they will be affected by the decisions you make.

→ If you could change one thing about the way [e.g., you get the budget from us], what would it be?

→ If we changed the formatting on this form a little, it would save us time and still get your needs met. What do you say?

→ Customers are frustrated, because they think our right hand doesn't know what the left hand is doing. I have some ideas about how we can get in sync, and I'd like to hear yours.

→ If the admins from our two departments got together regularly, it would help everyone in both departments.

→ There are ways we could have coordinated better in the last project. Let's learn from them for next time.

→ [Department] has a different perspective on this. Why not talk to them before you get too far into it, to avoid surprises on down the line?

Perfect Phrases to Get Office Members to Work Collaboratively

You see it when others may not. Even within departments, people can exclude others who could be resources and are stakeholders. For example, technical people often have their own software biases and reject suggestions from people who don't share their preferences, or they forget the concerns of the end user. When you sense that turf building is interfering with effectiveness, invite collaboration.

→ I'm not on anyone's side here. There aren't sides in this. We're on the same team. I'm trying to help everyone remember that.

→ I'm hearing some competitiveness. I think if we were less concerned with being right, we'd spark each other's genius.

→ I know we don't see eye-to-eye on this—which is why I suggest we include each other in planning. It will be easier to adapt to each other's needs now.

→ I'm concerned that if we don't give [colleague] a heads-up on this, he may stand in the way later on.

→ This would work a lot better if you get the stakeholders on board before it goes too far for their input to matter.

→ Let's each take a piece of this project so we all have a stake in the outcome.

→ If we can start to define each person's contribution before we begin, the entire process will flow better. Let's look at what we're each inspired to do and then at our various skills.

→ Instead of shooting each other's ideas down, let's explore the logic behind the suggestions and build on that.

→ [Name] is good at marketing, and you know the numbers. It would be great for you to work together.

→ Can I circulate a memo about [initiative] so we can get input early on?

→ Are you keeping [name] in the loop on that? He has a stake in this.

→ If it were my project, I'd take [name] to lunch and pick her brain. She could really save a lot of wheel reinvention.

→ Why are you working alone? I can give you a list of people who would love to help.

Perfect Phrases to Encourage and Empower Office Members to Be Self-Sufficient

This section may seem to contradict the previous one, but it doesn't. Collaboration involves tapping into others' skills, talents, and support to complement each other. It's not about using others to do things you should and could be doing for yourself. Among the best things parents can do for their children is to give them roots and give them wings. You wisely do the same in an office situation. Encourage collaboration when the situation calls for it, but empower office members to be self-sufficient when they should be.

→ I can do the job for you, but I'd rather give you pointers so it will still be your baby.

→ What have you tried so far?

→ I spend a lot of time doing things for people that they could do much more quickly on their own once they learn how. I'm happy to help you learn how to do this.

→ I'll show you where to look that up.

→ The technology scared me at first, but it's simple now that I've learned it. I'll teach you so you won't have to stop what you're doing to get me involved.

→ You can do this. I'll walk you through it the first time.

→ You're going to *love* knowing how to do this once I show you.

→ The old expression "If you hear, you forget; if you do, you remember" applies here. Let me walk you through the steps so you'll remember for next time.

→ This will look good on your résumé. I can show you a sample from last year.

→ You don't need me. Give it a try on your own, and if you get stuck, come back this afternoon and we'll run through it.

→ You'll want to learn this yourself. You can apply it to so many other things.

→ Give yourself some credit here! I'll give you a pep talk. You can do it!

Perfect Phrases to Address Company Layoffs and Terminations

It's tough watching family, friends, and colleagues lose their jobs and go through the process of rebuilding self-esteem and careers. It's also hard for the survivors. Healing requires a delicate balance of walking through emotions while moving forward. It doesn't work to pretend that nothing happened or everything is OK (as much as many managers wish it would). Here are some phrases you can incorporate to help managers handle layoffs skillfully and to help coworkers move through the guilt, fear, and shock to refocus on company goals.

➜ (To manager) The staff is reeling from the layoffs. We need to let them grieve before we push them to move forward.

➜ (To manager) We know the recent rounds of firing were necessary. Still, it stings. It will help if you address what we're all feeling, so we can move through it.

➜ (To manager) People are in shock and need information. It will help if you communicate with the group.

➜ (To manager) People are angry and need opportunities to vent. They need to know you care about them.

➜ (To manager) People are anxious and need clear direction and a sense of purpose. Can you give them that?

➜ (To manager) People are grieving and feeling hopeless. They need your support.

➜ This is a tough time for us. We need each other more than ever.

➜ It's weird not having [name] here anymore. We don't need to pretend it's not. Let's be honest about how we feel and move forward.

➜ Now's the time to demonstrate our professionalism. Our managers need us more than ever.

➜ We're not sitting ducks waiting to be picked off here. To keep our jobs into the future, it's up to us to develop our skills, see what's needed and do what we can, and make ourselves indispensable.

→ I notice the people who are still here are the ones who made themselves valuable by [action]. Let's increase our own job security by being proactive.

→ We can be honest about how we feel and still step up to the plate and make this work.

→ Negative talk against management isn't getting us any-where. This was a difficult decision for them, I'm sure. Let's get behind them and all work as a team.

→ I feel guilty still having my job, but I'm going to trust man-agement that this needed to be done and stay focused.

→ I know we wish things were different, but we play the hand we've been dealt—and play it well.

Perfect Phrases to Manage Emotions

Emotions are natural human responses. When we manage them, we come across as sincere and powerful. When they manage us, we come across as unprofessional. These phrases tap into the power of emotion without seeming childlike. Part of creating a positive office culture is to encourage others to manage their emo-tions productively as well. Suppressed emotions create emotional land mines, which add to tension. Managed emotions energize.

→ I understand you're angry about this. I'm afraid you may do something you'll regret. I'd like to see you do some-thing constructive with your anger.

→ I notice that a lot of people are scared by what's happen-ing these days. I also notice that some are excited and energized by it and doing their best work. They're the ones I'm taking my cues from.

→ I can understand why you may feel resentful about [e.g., being bypassed]. I'd hate for that to sabotage your success here. How can you respond productively?

→ I realize I'm reacting to what you just said. I want to respond appropriately and need time for that.

→ I'm angry about that, and I want to make sure it doesn't happen again.

→ This is a surprise for me. I need a few minutes to reflect so I don't give a knee-jerk emotional response.

→ I'm crying because I feel strongly about this. Please ignore my tears and focus on the facts.

→ I brought Kleenex with me because I suspect I'll need it. However, my tears do not affect my ability to think rationally.

→ I won't pretend that how this was handled doesn't hurt. It does. I will deal with my upset.

→ I have to say I'm disappointed. I thought you would show me more courtesy in this matter, and it saddens me that [e.g., you bypassed me here]. How can I [e.g., be included in the future]?

→ I am shaken by the layoffs and would appreciate some assurances about our direction.

→ I'm upset, and I need more information to move through this. What went into this decision?

→ I'm stunned, and I don't know what to say. Please let me take some time to reflect.

CHAPTER 13

Perfect Phrases to Speak for Your Manager

There is a fine line between representing and upstaging your manager. Don't let that fact cause you to play small. Your manager needs you to be effective when you speak on his or her behalf.

Clients often demand to speak to the "boss," even when the exec turns right around to get the information from the admin. Vendors can see admins as a barrier to the exec rather than an ally managing the smooth flow of information to and from the manager's suite. Similarly, when you're sent on a quest at the direction of your manager, colleagues may not give you the same respect and cooperation they would give your manager. When you represent your manager, you act as a surrogate. Be an articulate, credible, and confident representative.

Can you as an admin effectively establish your position of representing and speaking on behalf of the person in charge? Will you ever be seen as the spokesperson you are without having to defend yourself? Also, can you respond to criticisms and assaults on your manager in ways that show both your loyalty and understanding of the complainant? Yes, yes, and yes!

It's a bit like being a translator. Translators relay the exact message in language the listener can understand without injecting their own opinions. They make judgment calls about wording based on their interpretation of the speaker's intent, not their own values.

It starts with self-confidence. Be the first to respect the importance of your role. Then, know the right things to do and say.

Just as speakers and audiences need to trust the authority and accuracy of translators, everyone you speak to on your manager's behalf needs to trust that when you speak for your manager, you have the credentials and skills to represent that person. That takes some well-honed phrases.

Perfect Phrases to Get Your Manager to Authorize You to Speak on His or Her Behalf

Clarify your authority to act on your manager's behalf. That knowledge will give you the confidence to speak credibly and effectively. If there are areas where more authority to act independently would help the smooth operation of the office, ask for it. Here are some perfect phrases to get your manager to sanction your role of manager stand-in when it is appropriate.

→ I know these calls are a nuisance. Why not let me handle them? I know you well enough that I can manage them the same way you would.

→ In the past, this task fell to me. Shall we go back to that? I know how you like it done.

→ I have that information at my fingertips; you'd have to dig for it. Would you like me to provide the information when people call with inquiries?

→ Since these requests ultimately come back to me anyway, can I go ahead and deal with them as I screen your calls? It would save us both time.

→ I'd be glad to attend and make the presentation on your behalf. I'm very familiar with it, since I created the Power-Point version.

→ I don't like to interrupt you for approval about [situation]. If you could authorize me to act on your behalf next time that happens, I wouldn't have to waste your time.

→ If you'd like, I can give out that information for you. That would save you from having to deal with an unscheduled visitor.

→ In [department], they handle these situations by delegating it to the admin. Shall we follow suit?

→ I can screen out the routine questions and answer them, freeing up more time for you. I'll holler if I have anything I'm unsure of. Sound good?

→ That's way below your pay grade, you know. Can I help?

Perfect Phrases to Get Your Manager to Stop Undermining Your Authority

Habits die hard, and your manager may sabotage your effort to represent him or her without realizing it. If that happens, call on these phrases to address it.

→ We agreed I'd be the go-to person about [area]. To help communicate that, will you refer people back to me when they go directly to you?

→ I know the staff is used to going to you for [area]. While it seems more efficient for you to just take care of it, if you refer them back to me, they'll get used to coming to me instead, and it will save everyone time in the long run. Will you do that?

→ It seems you give me authority and take it back. That means I really don't have it, because everyone knows you may contradict me. If you're not comfortable giving me authority in certain areas, let's just say so, and I'll represent you in more limited ways where I know you'll back me up.

→ I've got it handled. Is there something I've done that makes you hesitant to let me represent you here? How can I gain your trust?

→ Oh no you don't! You put me in charge of that, remember?

→ If you want people to trust me as your representative, back me up! I make decisions the way I think you want. When you contradict me or undo what I set in motion, it signals to people that I really don't represent you.

→ I notice you blamed me for [manager's mistake]. I want to support you, and I'm concerned that if I take the responsibility for errors I don't make, people won't trust me when I take steps on your behalf.

Perfect Phrases to Get Your Manager to Credential You to the Rest of the Office

Even if you have your manager's full confidence to speak on his or her behalf, you may want your manager to assure others of your role in that regard. Here are your phrases.

→ It's important for the staff to hear directly from you that I speak on your behalf. Will you announce that?

→ Since you've been the deciding voice in the past on this, they should hear from you that I speak with your authority now.

→ Your staff is used to taking direction from you. Can you tell everyone I handle [area] now?

→ When people ask you about [item], can you tell them I handle it? That way they'll get used to my having the authority in this.

→ I heard about an admin whose manager told the staff that when she opens her mouth, his voice comes out. Could you do that for me?

→ Before you leave, please send a memo out to the team telling them I am handling things for you in your absence.

Perfect Phrases to Get Others to Come Directly to You

You and your exec may understand your role in speaking on the exec's behalf, but it may not be as clear to or accepted by others. People like dealing with the person at the top, thinking it will get them what they want and need—fast. In truth, people can get a quicker (and sometimes more accurate) response if they deal with the one who is readily available and knows where to go to get any kind of information (both inside and outside the department). Often that's the admin. Here are some perfect phrases for getting folks to work with you instead of trying to work around you.

→ [Manager's name] has asked me to handle all these inquiries. So, let me help you now.

→ I can transfer you to [manager's name], but she'll send you right back to me. I'm the one who has the information you're looking for.

→ I'm not authorized to transfer you to [manager's name] on this. I am authorized to handle it.

→ I am here at [manager's name's] request (or direction).

→ I will be representing [manager's name] at this meeting today, since she can't come. And yes, I have the authority to decide on her behalf.

→ This function has been delegated to me. What do you need?

→ [Manager's name] doesn't handle these calls. I'll be glad to help you.

→ I do this now.

→ Picture me as [e.g., blond and with a moustache . . . describe your manager]. Pretend I'm he, because I'm here in the same capacity.

→ When I open my mouth, [manager's name's] voice comes out.

→ I speak with the full authority of [manager's name]. I know, I know: pretty exciting, huh!

→ [Manager's name] asked me to respond for her. She thought it was more efficient than calling you herself and then asking me for the info, since this is part of my job now.

→ This is my bailiwick.

→ Can you tell me what it's regarding? That way if I can handle it for her, I will.

→ I'm sorry; he'll be unavailable for the next few days. I believe I can help you.

→ I can get [manager's name] on the line for you, but he'll just refer you back to me. I handle [area].

→ [Manager's name] used to have this information, but now I do. What do you need?

→ I can provide you with the information or leave a message for [manager's name]. It may be as long as a week before she'll be able to get back to you. She's immersed in a big project.

→ [Manager's name] calls me his right-hand admin. That's because I can look up anything for you in a matter of minutes. What exactly do you need?

Perfect Phrases to Gracefully Inform Someone of Your Manager's Mistakes

Even though we all make mistakes, it can be a bit sticky letting others know that your manager messed up. You don't want your manager to lose face, nor do you want to besmirch his or her reputation. Before you tell the world when your manager blows it, ask how he or she would like for you to comment on errors. Your manager may prefer you to be up-front about it. Or not. Once you know, here are some ways to handle the situation so everybody comes out looking good.

→ I'm following up. The numbers have been revised.

→ I believe you were told [information], but the latest information is [correction].

→ [Manager's name] wanted me to double-check her figures, and there have been a couple of changes.

→ [Manager's name] told me to tell you she really botched [area] and needs to [correction].

→ [Manager's name] apologizes for the error and asked me to set the record straight.

→ I need to take back the monthly report. We have a few corrections.

→ Before you input these numbers, let me give it a second look.

→ The quote has changed from what you were told.

→ [Manager's name] asked me to tell you about some changes in the information.

→ It is taking a bit longer than he projected. I assure you, the result will be worth the wait.

→ It isn't like [manager's name] to [e.g., forget an appointment]. I'm sure if she's not here, something outside her control happened.

Perfect Phrases to Make Your Manager Look Good

When an admin sings a manager's praises, people notice. It inspires confidence in your manager for the word to get around that you like and respect your exec. After all, you have the insider's view of what your manager is really like. You're not "sucking up" when you share attributes you truly admire about your exec whenever you can.

→ Whatever he does, you can be sure he'll give it 100 percent.

→ You will love working with her! She's the best!

→ He's my mentor, and I couldn't have a better one!

→ You're going to be so pleased with this proposal. [Manager's name] spent a lot of time on it—getting all the information you'll need.

→ I really like working with her. She's amazing.

→ I have learned so much, working with him.

→ I couldn't have a better manager.

→ I've been working with [manager's name] for [time span] now, and I keep discovering more to like and admire. For example, [item].

Perfect Phrases to Address Complaints and Criticisms About Your Manager

Don't take sides when people complain about or criticize your manager. Here are some things you can say that will help you stay out of the fray, while showing empathy and loyalty.

→ If you have an issue with [manager's name], please deal with her directly. I'm happy to help you if there is something specific you need, but it wouldn't be appropriate for me to get in the middle of this.

→ I can't advise you on this except to suggest you turn your complaint into a request and bring it up with [manager's name] directly.

→ I find that when I have an issue, it helps for me to be very clear about what I want to have happen and focus on that when I talk about it. That could work for you with this situation.

→ Are you aware that the person you're criticizing so harshly is my employer, and we're a team?

→ Hmm . . . I don't know what happened, but let's make it right.

→ That's not the usual practice in this office. Let me take the information and see what happened so we can correct it.

→ I hear what you're saying, and I'm sorry for the hassle. I'll apologize for the department.

→ I'm glad you're sharing this. It's how we improve.

→ You'll have to ask [manager's name] about that—but it doesn't sound like him.

→ I'm sorry that happened. The best way to approach her is [approach].

→ What do you think happened? I haven't heard this complaint before.

→ I can understand why that upsets you. I find it easy to cut her slack for things like that because I see the big picture of all she does. But I can see why you'd be concerned. Thanks for telling me.

→ Thank you for stopping by. We don't hear this very often, but when we do, we like to correct any miscommunication.

CHAPTER 14

Perfect Phrases for Professionalism and Empowerment

Sometimes the titles Administrative Assistant, Office Manager, and even Executive Assistant lead people to put us in boxes we don't fit in . . . or keeps us in boxes we've outgrown. While respect for the administrative and office professions is growing (with thanks to the amazing professionals in the field and their advocates such as Susan and organizations such as IAAP), there still are plenty of people who haven't moved beyond the day when women became secretaries because they didn't want to teach or be nurses while they waited to get married. The position of secretary has come a long way and is now a highly skilled profession of choice that deserves respect.

Have you ever said, "I'm just the assistant" to explain your inability to handle something? I ask my audiences for a show of hands on that question, and enough hands shoot up to be scary. Your role as an assistant may indeed be the reason why you're not the one to handle certain requests—but the word *just* implies that the issue is one of status and professionalism, not of scope.

You represent your profession and are in charge of your own professionalism. If you want to be seen as a professional, you have to be one. If you want to be treated as a professional, you have to respect yourself first and then inspire respect from others. Keep up with your profession and seek continuous improvement. It's up to you to evaluate your strengths and weaknesses and update your skills.

This chapter gives you the perfect phrases for taking charge of your career and professionalism by standing up for yourself and your chosen profession, requesting and independently seeking ongoing education and training, asking for and assuming more responsibilities, and establishing your worth by achieving professional certification. All these actions will empower you to achieve the career dreams you have for yourself.

Perfect Phrases to Determine and Expand Your Empowerment Level

Power is the ability to act. Empowerment is enablement. Power can be imposed. Empowerment is based on agreement. Your job title and responsibilities afford you power in some areas. Your collaborative agreements expand that power into empowerment that will help you be effective on behalf of your company, your manager, and yourself. To help achieve that goal, take advantage of these useful phrases.

→ My job description empowers me to [description]. I interpret that to mean I can [authority—e.g., change vendors when advisable].

→ I am responsible for [responsibility]. To be able to carry that out, I'd like the authority to [e.g., speak directly to the CEO]. Will that work for you?

→ There are a few people who ignore my requests for [e.g., properly submitted expense reports]. The recourse I have now is to tell you, and that feels so high school. I'd like to [action] so that staff knows [e.g., everyone has to fill the reports out accurately]. Will you empower me to do that?

→ (To manager) Having to [e.g., come to you for routine approvals] is an inefficient use of our time. I'd like to have the authority to [specific request—e.g., approve routine items myself].

→ I'm in charge of [e.g., facilitating this meeting], and I have the following protocol: [guidelines]. That means I'll stop you if you [action—e.g., get off topic].

→ I can help you [goal—e.g., stay on schedule] if you want me to. I'll just need you to support me when I [e.g., let you know it's time to move on].

→ (To manager) To keep you on schedule, I plan to come get you if the meeting runs over. It's my job to keep you on schedule. Agree?

Perfect Phrases to Establish Peer Regard with Your Manager's Colleagues

Your manager's colleagues' names are likely to appear higher than yours on some organizational chart. That doesn't mean these people can or should pull rank, show disrespect, or dismiss your expertise in their dealings with you. Every situation is different, of course. Sometimes tasks such as getting people coffee are legitimate team activities, and other times they are diminishments that betray your professionalism. Set boundaries as appropriate, staying aware of your own role in establishing peer regard.

→ We have lines of authority in the org chart, and yet we're on the same team in the project. It's a balancing act for us—that's really about getting the job done.

→ I honor your position. This isn't about rank. I'm trying to get the job done, and I need your help to do that.

→ Like you, I have a job to do, and you're a key player in my ability to do my job. You'll work with me, won't you?

→ Just so you know, I take my responsibility to [e.g., keep my manager on schedule] seriously. That means I will come get you if the meeting runs over. It's my job to do that.

→ I'm the project leader on this. That means I will be assigning tasks to you. Weird, I know, since you're way higher on the org chart!

→ I respect your expertise. Please respect mine, which is administration. I'm really interested in helping everyone's projects run smoothly—including yours.

→ Are you pulling rank on me here? Because I'm not speaking on my own authority; I speak on my manager's authority.

→ I find that remark incredibly dismissive. You do know that I'm a skilled professional, don't you?

→ I'd be happy to [e.g., get coffee] for you if it didn't interfere with [e.g., my need to be present at this meeting].

→ The admins don't get people coffee anymore—we're all getting our own. The coffee thing interfered with the rest of our responsibilities.

→ Have you been watching too much "Mad Men" on TV? It's a different world now.

→ I'll do that this time as a team member to support our efforts here, since I see that it will move things along. Next time, I'd like us to make other arrangements so I won't be taking time away from my job priorities.

Perfect Phrases to Get Others to Respect Your Profession

It's hard to get respect for your professionalism from people who don't respect your profession. I'm sure you know that not everyone has what it takes to be an office professional. Increase the general regard of your profession by speaking highly of it, referencing what it takes to be an office professional, and being openly proud of what you do.

→ I always wanted to be a secretary from when I was a child. Now I'm an admin, and it's all I dreamed of and more.

→ People sometimes say, "You're so smart; why are you an admin instead of a manager?" I reply, "You answered your own question."

→ I love being an office professional, because [reason].

→ Why do you put the word *just* in front of *admin* and ask if I'm *just* an admin? I'm actually not just anything. I'm a professional with a broad scope of expertise.

→ I respect your profession and what you do, and I am so glad to be in my profession doing what I do.

→ I had no idea there was so much involved in my profession. I'm amazed at the things I get to do.

→ My profession is changing so fast that I have to work to stay on top of it.

→ I was researching [area—e.g., establishing virtual teams] in [professional resource—e.g., *OfficePro* magazine] and found an article that explains [main point].

→ Just so you know, my [professional conference—e.g., IAAP convention] has sessions on the exact challenges we've been talking about at this meeting. That's one of the reasons why I'll be there.

→ Let me know if there are specific sessions you want me to attend at my admin conference. I can bring back the latest info.

→ My professional association is forming [e.g., a Web community/eGroups/a resource library]. I think it would be a good model for us here.

→ I've been asked to join a product focus group for [company that produces the product] at this year's conference. They like to get input from end-user professionals, such as admins.

→ I'm amazed at how much of the same ground our professional association conferences cover. We should compare notes when we both get back.

Perfect Phrases to Get Others to Respect Your Professionalism

Garnering respect for the admin profession gives you a solid foundation toward getting respect for your own professionalism. You also increase your professional regard by acting like a professional, offering professional opinions, and displaying competence. At times, you make a straightforward request for it.

→ In my industry, they look at it this way.

→ I have a professional opinion about that.

→ Wow. I'd like to [e.g., notarize that for you], but it would violate my professional code of ethics.

→ In my profession, there is a saying that [saying].

→ I was reading about the changes in my profession in the past five years and thinking—wow—that would be scary if it weren't exciting!

→ [Software—e.g., Office 2010] has become standard in my industry now.

→ Let me run that by my colleagues.

→ I'm the admin and the project leader.

→ Thanks for the compliment. I didn't learn all this by accident. I've been keeping up with my profession.

→ I am a professional, and I do expect to be treated as one.

→ I respect your professionalism, and I ask you to respect mine.

Perfect Phrases to Get Others to Refer to Your Position Appropriately

Outdated stereotypes and politically incorrect terminology often live on in the workplace. Some people don't realize the implications—others are just plain rude. Here are some phrases for handling both groups.

→ I am [manager's name's] executive assistant. I don't go by "girl"; I go by [how you like to be called].

→ You must have me mixed up with someone else. I am the Marketing Department Coordinator.

→ This position was upgraded to [title].

→ Be careful: that term dates you. The title we use today is [title].

→ Do you refer to other administrative professionals that way? If you do, I suspect you're alienating a few with that term. That term is considered a put-down these days. I'm sure you don't mean it that way.

→ I prefer that you call me by my real title, [how you like to be called].

→ My manager refers to me as her administrative professional. I did hear her tell someone if she had to choose between me and her right arm, it would be tough.

→ Would you like my business card so you can remember how to refer to me?

→ You have my title wrong. I am [title].

→ I deserve more credit. I am [title].

→ I do a lot more than that. I am [title].

→ Tell you what. Let's refer to each other by our proper titles. Mine is [title].

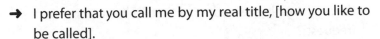

Perfect Phrases to Request Advanced Training or Education

In today's fast-paced office, no one can rest on past laurels. We have to gain new skills and keep improving. Here's how you can ask for and get more training—to take your career to the next level. Note: while it's a boon when others pay for your training, be willing to invest in yourself. It's your career. Plus, when managers see you investing in your advancement, they may decide to contribute after all.

→ We're dealing with these [specific] problems in the office. This [product/conference/class] will give us solutions. Do I have your approval to [buy it/attend]?

→ During my annual review, we talked about my gaining skills in [area]. I found a [class/conference/training course] that will enable me to do just that. Will you approve my [request]?

→ I need to learn [skill] in order to [function]. Here's how I can get the skills I need.

→ Will you support my attending [training]? Here's how it will make me a better admin.

→ You'd like me to [function] to free you up to [priority]. This [product/training/class] will give us both what we need.

→ Most people, including me, are using only a small fraction of [software]. There's a class at [location] that will help me use all the bells and whistles.

→ If I can go to [conference], I can bring back the information and train the other admins. You'd get five people trained for the price of one.

→ As lead admin, I need to be a role model for the others. This [training] will impact the whole office.

→ The next big trend in [area] is [skill]. If you'll approve my taking this class, we can get a leg up on [skill].

→ I know my professional conference attendance doesn't fit in our budget. It's important enough to me for me to invest in it myself. Will you approve the time off?

Perfect Phrases to Ask for Support in Obtaining Professional Certification

Certification is the hallmark of a professional. To receive certification, you have to earn it, and that means developing professional skills that you might not have explored without it. Certification verifies what you know and what you're capable of. It can also make a difference when you're vying for a promotion, a salary increase, or more responsibility. Here's how to ask for support to achieve this worthy goal.

→ In your area, [specific certification] is the pinnacle of professionalism. The [specific] certification is the standard of excellence in mine. I'd like to pursue it. Will you support me?

→ I want the challenge of achieving the [specific] certification. Will you approve this request for study materials and the exam fee?

→ The [college/chapter] has started a review course for the [specific certification] exam. I'd like to take it and get certified. Can this be part of my professional goal as we discussed at my last performance review?

→ The [specific] certification covers [areas]. Mastering this information would make me a better admin for the department. Will you approve my registering for the exam in May?

→ The [specific] certification content nicely parallels what I do here at [company]. I'd like to test my knowledge and sit for the exam. Will you cover the exam fee and study materials? I'll do you proud.

→ Someone at my level here should have professional certification. Can we make this part of my professional goals for [year]?

→ I'd like to start a review course for the [specific] certification for admins here at [company]. I have an instructor committed. Will you be our champion and help us get the cost covered by [source]?

→ Things change so fast in every profession. I'd like to pursue certification to keep up and stay ahead. Can I get you to sign here to approve my taking the [specific] certification exam?

→ You know how I like a challenge. The [specific] certification is a big one but doable. What would you say if I asked to study and sit for the [specific] certification?

→ My colleagues have been encouraging me to obtain the [specific] certification. Can we make it part of my professional objectives?

→ All the professionals here have certifications to show they're tops in their field. I'm ready for that myself. During my review, you indicated that I'll be taking on more responsibilities with no more pay. In lieu of a raise, I'd like support for getting certified. Can you do that for me?

→ I want to stretch myself and learn new skills. How would you feel about my getting certified in [area]?

→ Like you, I want and need to keep up with my profession. That's why I am requesting that you approve my certification in [area].

→ I can see that very soon, I'll be asked to [requirement]. That's part of the [specific] certification. Will you help me to get ready for the new assignment by allowing me to get certified in [area]?

→ Every profession has its standard of excellence. The Certified Administrative Professional rating is the standard for admins, just as the Certified Speaking Professional is the hallmark for speaking professionals and Project Management Professional is the standard for project managers. Will you approve my getting this certification?

CHAPTER 15

Perfect Phrases for Career Management

There's a saying that those who can't *do* teach. It's not as clearly stated, but many people seem to erroneously believe that those who can't *manage* assist. The office administrator role is a profession of choice that is preferred by many competent professionals who love what they do and have no desire to manage, lead, or "move up" the hierarchy.

Whether this is or isn't you, this chapter on career management is still for you. You don't have to want to change jobs to benefit from career management phrases.

Great careers don't happen by accident. They're a result of planning, preparing, and both creating and recognizing opportunities. Savvy admins don't think of themselves as victims of circumstance. They don't make their jobs smaller to fit themselves; they make themselves bigger to fit—not just their jobs as described but also as business trends indicate. They think of themselves as miners and masters of opportunity.

Don't let the magic fade from your career. Discover the power you have to develop exciting new opportunities.

What have you done today to move yourself toward a more fulfilling career? These phrases will help you advance.

Perfect Phrases to Identify Your Career Path

The first step to establishing a successful career is to define a career path that builds on your interests and strengths. Of course, no one knows your interests as well as you do. Still, guidance can help you see skills and talents you might have missed and opportunities you hadn't considered. Moreover, knowing that you think in terms of a career path can change how others view your professionalism. It will alert them to keep their eyes open for possibilities.

The world is changing so quickly that no path will be a straight line—but support and focus will help you progress. Here are examples of how to invite collaboration on your career path.

→ I'm assessing my skills to see what career options I have. What would you say are my greatest strengths?

→ I love doing [task/project]. What career options do you think would capitalize best on my passion?

→ I'd love to have a job like yours. How would I prepare myself for that role?

→ Where could someone with my skill set go within the organization?

→ What do you see as the next step for me in my career progression?

→ I'm interested in [skill set] and [skill set]. Where could I use both of these?

→ What would it take for me to [e.g., move into the training area] and one day become [e.g., an instructor for technology skills]?

→ What are the drawbacks of being a [profession]?

→ If you had it to do all over again, would you choose the same career path? Why or why not?

→ If you had it to do all over again, what steps would you take to prepare yourself for the future?

→ What jobs are most sought after?

Perfect Phrases to Request Strategic and Interesting Assignments

Don't wait for someone to offer you interesting assignments to further your career. Think strategically. Look ahead to where you're going, and discern the skills you need to get there. Some assignments won't move you forward. Others will. Step up and ask for experiences that further develop your skills and expand your professional networks. That could even mean inventing projects no one else had considered.

→ One of my goals this year is to [develop/expand] my skills in [area]. How would you feel about my taking over this [assignment/project]?

→ In my performance review, we agreed I'd bolster my skills in [area]. This assignment seems like a great place to start.

→ If I were involved in [project], it would help me in [career goal]. Do I have your support to join the project group?

→ It's been a goal of mine to [goal]. This project is a perfect way for me to learn the skills from the inside out. Shall I sign up for it?

→ I've always wanted to [task]. Can I take over this assignment? I know I'll do a great job, because I'm so motivated.

→ I have a great idea that would [enhance productivity/save money/improve communications]. I'd like to brainstorm the idea and lead the project if you agree that it would be productive.

Perfect Phrases to Tie Your Job Functions into Your Career Path

Don't make the mistake of seeing your job functions only in terms of the immediate task at hand. Tie everything you do into the broader vision of your career path.

→ There are several job titles that accurately reflect my responsibilities, but I think since we're positioning me in the direction of [job], the best one would be [proposed title].

→ This year I'd like my role [e.g., at the conference] to include [task—e.g., managing registration], because it will allow me to meet a lot of people and put me in a great position to [e.g., run the conference] next year.

→ I can learn the technology for [task/project] in a couple of days. I know it's not cost effective for me to do that for this project alone, but the skills I learn will transfer to [task aligned with career objective].

→ I'd like to expand my duties to include [duty]. By being responsible for the whole process, I can better understand and control the flow.

→ I don't mind [task—e.g., taking notes at the meeting for you]. I learn a lot that will be useful for me to know in the future.

→ The reason why I like to [task that may seem to waste your skills—e.g., get the board members coffee] is that [advantage—e.g., it promotes networking].

→ If I'm going to be able to represent you in [area], it would make sense for me to [e.g., be copied on related e-mails].

Perfect Phrases to Tie Your Career Goals into Your Manager's Best Interests

Watch out for sounding as if you're just in it for yourself. Balance your career goals, strategies, and requests with your genuine interest in serving your exec and company.

→ I know you're positioned to be the next new [title]. Let me handle some of your current responsibilities so that when you move up, I can cover for you here and the department won't miss a beat.

→ Being indispensable is advantageous, but I'm concerned that someone in the executive suite is going to want to snatch you up, and I'm concerned about how the company would replace you. It could really free you up to know I can cover for you in any transition.

→ You know I'm ambitious, and there are so many things I want to learn and do. I hope you also know that when I set my priorities, I look for ways to develop that serve your needs too—not just my goals.

→ I talked to some admins who say their managers feel threatened by their expertise and try to hold them back. I'm glad you know that I apply everything I do to our mutual success (or to your success).

→ I'm glad you're not threatened by my ambitions.

Perfect Phrases to Position Yourself for Promotions

Promotions don't just happen. They're the result of career management. If you don't position yourself to reach the next level, someone who does will be the one to get the promotion that could have been yours.

→ I'm working hard so that one day I can move into [new position]. I'm using you as my role model.

→ I know that [name] will be retiring in a year. I'd like to learn elements of her position to be considered for her replacement and train people to do my job.

→ [Tasks] are for a higher pay grade. I'd like to do them anyway—so I can learn, and so it will be easier for you to sell the execs on my promotion next year.

→ I'd like to better use my [degree/certification/talents]. Will you support me if I apply for the open position in marketing?

Perfect Phrases to Request a Raise or More Responsibilities

If you sit and wait for someone to notice your contributions and then respond with a promotion or pay increase, you'll wait a long time. It's a do-it-yourself world. Ask for what you need to move your career ahead. Here are some phrases for you to start the ball rolling. You can get more phrases in Chapter 8, Perfect Phrases to Make Requests and Negotiate.

→ I prepared a draft of an updated job description to reflect all the new things I have taken on. Can we talk about it?

→ I'm ready to take on the responsibilities of [area]. Will you give me the chance?

→ OfficeTeam does an annual salary guide, and my pay is way below the average for [title/job responsibilities]. How can I get up to par?

→ I want to position myself for a raise by adding value to my job contributions. I'd like to take on some responsibilities from the next pay grade so that at my next review I'll be contributing at a higher level and positioned well for a promotion.

→ I want to use all my talents on the job. I could do that by [task].

→ This salary increase is less than I expected. Can we schedule a six-month review to relook at my responsibilities and pay?

→ I understand that salaries are capped. But to reward me for my additional responsibilities, what about a bonus?

→ I found out my salary isn't keeping pace with the level of responsibilities I've been assigned and my contributions to the bottom line. We need to fix that!

Perfect Phrases to Get a Manager to Give You Due Credit

Some office cultures consider it the norm for the leaders and managers to take credit for work primarily done by admins and office pros. Sometimes you score points with your own manager by allowing that custom to continue. There're other times when your omission might not have been deliberate. Know when getting recognition is important enough to ask for it.

→ I'd really like to have it noted in my performance review that I spearheaded this project.

→ Can I have my name on the list of contributors?

→ I've noted each team member's contribution in the final report. That way if people have questions or want to follow up, they'll know which of us to contact.

→ I was disappointed that my work on the [project] wasn't noted. Is there a reason you left me off the list?

→ One of my annual goals was to develop a procedures manual. I'd like my name on the cover. Can we do that?

→ I've copied all the team members on my suggestion—that way we'll all be on the same page.

→ Sometimes, I don't feel like an equal member of the team. Is there a reason my suggestions aren't noted as coming from me?

→ Since this was an original [concept/drawing] of mine, where should I put my name? In the same position as the other contributors?

→ It's important to me to receive credit for this contribution. I want to be able to add it to my professional vita.

→ Are you aware that the idea you shared at the meeting actually came from me? It's important to my career that people know my accomplishments.

→ This [report] is essentially mine. I see a few edits but don't understand why my name isn't on it.

Perfect Phrases to Network for Career Advancement

They say it's not what you know but whom you know. Actually, it's both. In addition to having excellent skills, the stronger and more widespread your professional network is, the better the position you're in to advance in your chosen field. That includes networking to get yourself on decision makers' radar and even the janitors', since you never can tell who could become the one to know. The hierarchy is flattening, and if you're reluctant to relate at every level, you'll miss a networking opportunity that others will embrace.

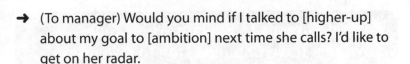

→ (To manager) Would you mind if I talked to [higher-up] about my goal to [ambition] next time she calls? I'd like to get on her radar.

→ (To manager) I thought I'd make a few comments to [higher-up] at the gathering about our [initiative]. Wouldn't hurt for him to hear from someone else how excited we are about it, would it?

→ (To higher-up) One of the things I love about working with my manager is that he supports my desire to [ambition].

→ (To janitor, etc.) How do you like us to let you know we need something?

→ (To janitor, etc.) I'm so grateful for what you do. Is there anything I can do to make your job easier?

→ I've enjoyed working with you, and I'd like to stay in touch [e.g., on LinkedIn]. May I add you to my contacts?

→ Let me get your card. I have information that will help you with your project.

→ I'd love to take you to lunch and noodle a bit.

→ I've wanted to talk with someone who [what this person does]. You never know how we can help each other.

→ It sounds as if I can help you with [area], and in turn, you can help me [action/goal].

→ I like to get to know all kinds of people. We never know when we start talking how we can support each other. It's often surprising to discover opportunities.

→ It's been a while since we last corresponded, and I don't want to lose touch with you. I'm checking in to stay connected.

Perfect Phrases to Explain When Your Loyalties Have Changed Due to Promotion

You can't move forward to new things without leaving some of the old things behind. This reality can be unsettling when your move is a promotion and you have to leave some of the old colleagues, behaviors, and loyalties to accommodate the new. Here are some perfect phrases to handle the transition with grace and class.

➜ I miss seeing and talking to you all, but my new job is keeping me hopping.

➜ I was able to share that kind of information in my old position, but with my new job, I'm afraid that's confidential.

➜ I wish I could support your project, but the new criterion I'm working under is very specific, and I don't believe your project fits the guidelines. I'm sorry.

➜ I'm sorry that I haven't been able to meet for lunch the way we used to do. My schedule changed, and I don't have the free time I used to have. I miss you.

➜ To be honest, my focus is now more on [area], so I'm not keeping up with [other area] as well as I used to.

➜ With the new job, I look at the situation differently now.

➜ I'd love to be able to help you out, but my [schedule/commitments] just won't let me. Sorry, I can't give my usual input.

➜ I wish I could help you out and do the report for you, but I'm immersed in all the new things I have to learn. I'll jump-start you by [way].

→ (To former manager) I wish I could help you more with the specifics of my old job, but I am swamped with all I have to do here. Have my replacement call if she gets stuck on something after reading the instructions I left behind.

Perfect Phrases to Find a Good Mentor and Develop a Mutually Rewarding Relationship

Every professional needs a sounding board in the form of a mentor. A good mentor will help you identify your strengths, face your weaknesses, and discover ways to fill the gap between the two; share experiences that you can learn from without undergoing the hard knocks yourself; cheerlead when you need some support; and tell you things you need to know that others won't about your style and prospects for success. Here are some perfect phrases for getting that perfect career mentor.

→ I admire how you [strength] so much. I'd like to learn about [skill you want to develop] from you. Will you mentor me?

→ I study how you [skill]. I learn from watching you, and I wonder if you'd be willing to mentor me.

→ In my performance review, I listed getting a mentor as my top goal. You're my first choice because [reason]. Can I sign you up for the job?

→ I playfully tell people that when I grow up, I want to be just like you. Someone suggested I ask you to mentor me, and bells went off. Will you?

→ I know asking someone to mentor is a big request. I take it very seriously. If you would do that for me, I would put your wisdom and guidance to good use.

→ I'd like to start a mentoring program here at work and develop some guidelines. Would you help me establish a mentoring program by serving as my mentor, the first mentor, the one who helps establish the program?

Perfect Phrases to Gracefully Leave a Job, a Manager, or a Work Team

Nothing is forever. When the time comes to move out of one situation and into another, be gracious and don't burn bridges. With today's work flux, someone you leave behind at one organization can easily turn up as your new manager at another. The moral: develop, build, and maintain good relationships with everyone who passes through your life.

→ I can't tell you how sorry I am to be leaving the work team. I'm excited about the new experience, but I'll really miss everyone here.

→ I have learned so much from you. You've really been a boost to my career. Thanks for all you've done and for being such a great role model.

→ I have so enjoyed working here. But this offer was too good to refuse. It's the next step on my career path.

→ I know you've been through this yourself . . . leaving one job to start another. It's bittersweet.

→ I have everyone's contact information. When I come across opportunities for you, believe me, I'll pass the information on. I'll be a team member from afar.

→ Here's my new contact information. Let's stay in touch. Maybe we can discover some joint [projects/ventures].

→ I've learned a lot working with you. Thanks for all the [help/support/opportunities] you've given me over the years.

→ Feel free to call me if you need some insight on aspects of my former job. I'm willing to help get the new person settled in.

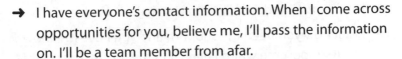

Perfect Phrases to Deal with a Demotion or Loss of Status

Every career has its ups and downs. It's not so much what happens but how you handle the situation and what you learn from it that really matters. Here are some perfect phrases for dealing with the low points in your professional life.

→ I understand why the decision was made, and I'm trying to stay positive. Can we talk about sweetening the situation some?

→ Yes, I do feel hurt right now. But I'm putting those feelings aside for the good of the work team.

→ I know this new job needs to be done, and I'll give it 100 percent. In the meantime, I hope you'll help me continue to develop my professional skills.

→ As the situation changes, I want to be considered for [area].

→ I'm disappointed, but I'll help you make it work.

→ Right now you need my support, and you have it. I know you'll support me when I need it in the future. That's what good teammates do for each other.

→ Since I'm making a backward career move, is there anything we can do to keep my career on target?

→ I know that you've given this a lot of thought and that the decision was difficult. Are there other challenges you could give me so I can continue to develop professionally?

Perfect Phrases to Address Getting Passed Over for a Promotion

When you are competing with others for a single opening, someone has to win it, while the others have to accept it and move on. But those who weren't chosen needn't be "losers." Here are some perfect phrases to show your team spirit, professionalism, and resilience.

→ (To successful candidate) I am disappointed, but as a team player, I want you to know you have my support.

→ (To successful candidate) Congratulations on the promotion. I wish we both could have been chosen. Know that I'll support you 100 percent.

→ (To manager) I wish that things had turned out differently. What can I do to improve my chances for next time?

→ (To manager) I wish I had been your first choice. What can I do to be considered the next time there's an opening?

→ (To manager) I accept your decision. In the meantime, I'll continue to develop new skills. Put my name down for the next job opening.

→ (To manager) Let's talk about what would have made me the best choice so that next time, I will be the most qualified applicant.

→ (To manager) Since I wasn't chosen for that position, where do you think I should put my energies in regard to my career path? Is there a better fit for me?

→ I lost this round, but I'll keep trying. You know me. I'm a go-getter.

→ (To manager) What were the deciding factors in choosing [name] over me? I'd like to address any deficiencies.

→ (To manager) To get the promotion next time, what skills or abilities do I need to hone?

Perfect Phrases to Get Support for Involvement in a Professional Association

A great way to establish powerful networks is through membership in a professional association. Talk about the value with management. Here are ways you can get your employer to support this vital career component.

→ I love my association meetings! Last night I [connected with name/learned information].

→ I'll call [name's] assistant. I know him from my IAAP meetings. He'll get you on [name's] calendar.

→ Just as you're a member of [association], for me to keep tabs on changes in my field, I need to be a member of my professional organization. Will you approve my membership dues?

→ Here are ten reasons why my being a member of [association] will directly benefit you and the company.[1]

→ I attended a program at [association] last night. I joined because it was so valuable to me. I thought about asking you to support the dues, but it was worth it to me to pay them myself. I will need your support in making sure I'm available to attend the meetings.

→ We each have a specialty. Mine is administration. To stay at the top of my game, I need a professional network. Will you support my involvement in [association]?

→ To keep pace with all the changes in my field, I need to be a member of [association]. Here's what it would involve. [Details.]

→ Here are three problems we're experiencing in the department, and here's how [association] can help me find workable solutions.

→ I'd like to share this [article/information] with you. As a member of [association], I'd get this kind of info on a regular basis. I need to become a member.

→ As a member of [association], I'd have access to thousands of administrative professionals throughout the world. Here's how that connection could help us. [Benefits.]

1. http://www.iaap-hq.org/membershiproi

Conclusion

Office Professionals Can't Afford to Play Small Anymore

The most certain thing in business these days is that it's changing. We meet, work with, and hear from admins and office pros with very different challenges, but one thing is constant: change.

We talk to people who struggle with the abnormal new normal and to others who thrive with opportunities from all the change. We see a lot of fear, and we see a lot of growth. We see some admins play defense, putting more attention on arguing about how things aren't their fault than on how to grow into the new demands. We see others respond proactively by laying, implementing, and adapting strategies and developing new skills to make themselves indispensable.

There are no guarantees. Nevertheless, speaking from our combined years of experience with admins, it's clear: the odds of success greatly favor those office professionals who won't allow themselves to collapse into fear and play small. If a manager must choose between retaining an admin who has made the job small enough to fit him or her and one who has made him- or herself big enough to fit the job, the odds favor the one who has grown into—and, as needed, beyond—the job description.

The name of the game is empowerment. You may need to ease into empowerment more slowly and choose phrases that don't challenge the status quo while you discover where and how status quo challenges aren't only possible but also needed. Or you may be ready to show up in your office with a more empowered approach tomorrow. It could be that you've made yourself as big as you need to be already but needed empowered language to express yourself. If so, we hope you found it here.

Whatever your level of professionalism and empowerment, we'd like to remind you of what Susan said in her author preface: you are amazing. If you didn't know that before you picked this book up, we hope you have a better sense of it now. We joke that admins should run the world, but in fact, you already do. We wish for our efforts here to help you do that in even bigger and more joyful and effective ways.

Resources

Meryl Runion provides a free newsletter, free webinars, and numerous articles on her website at www.speakstrong.com. She also responds directly to individual questions. She is available for in-house and Web-based communication training and facilitation. You can download her "Top Ten PowerPhrases for Admins" at www.speakstrong.com/admins.

IAAP offers newsletters and magazines such as *OfficePro* written just for you, your own certifications such as the Certified Administrative Professional (CAP), books, conferences, workshops, and desktop learning. Go to www.iaap-hq.org for information.

OfficeTeam offers complimentary guides, articles, and other materials to help administrative professionals develop their skills and excel in the workplace. Go to www.officeteam.com for career resources and online job search. To learn about the latest administrative hiring trends, skills and positions in demand, and salaries in the profession, visit the service's comprehensive Salary Center at www.officeteam.com/salarycenter.

Other Resources

Because Web communities and resources change so quickly, instead of listing them here, we recommend you find them on your own. Your favorite search engine is your best empowerment tool for this! There are hundreds and even thousands of communities waiting for you to join in. There are hundreds and even thousands of websites with answers to your specific questions. Give them a try.

About the Authors

Meryl Runion brings her experience from more than a thousand seminars around the world to this book. She is a Certified Speaking Professional and the author of eight books that have sold more than 350,000 copies worldwide. She loves to hike, learn, dance, and find better ways to say things.

Meryl works with administrative professionals at every level of organizations who are ready to step into a higher level of professionalism, empowerment, and collaborative communication.

You can contact Meryl at:

- ■ Website: www.speakstrong.com
- ■ Twitter: http://twitter.com/merylrunion
- ■ LinkedIn: www.linkedin.com/in/merylrunion
- ■ Facebook: www.facebook.com/speakstrong

Susan Fenner is the Manager of Education and Events at the International Association of Administrative Professionals (IAAP), with members throughout the world. She served as the Admin Support Advisor on Monster and has a column, "Turning Jobs into Careers," in *OfficePro* and another, "Work Smart," in *Office Solutions* magazine. She is General Editor for the *Complete Office Handbook* and coauthor of *Making Your Message Memorable:*

Communicating Through Stories. She originated a series of weekly podcasts for admins and developed the IAAP Options Office Skills and Options Tech Training Programs. Her passion is helping admins discover and reach their full potential—in life and the workplace.

You can contact Susan at sfenner@iaap-hq.org.